PRAISE FOR *DESIGI*

"A lot of what gets passed on as 'good careers advice' is based on 20th-century corporate careers. Real life is running somewhat ahead of this but few experts have been able to capture, distil and pass on what matters in today's always-online world – mostly because we are too old. *Design Your Life* is the book to fill that gap. Erifili is talking to her Gen Z peers, but her book is also a must-read for anyone who is curious to understand how we can make the most of our unique skills and qualities, while harnessing the exciting new tech-driven possibilities for a long-term and fulfilling working life." ISABEL BERWICK, HOST OF THE *FINANCIAL TIMES* PODCAST WORKING IT AND AUTHOR OF *THE FUTURE-PROOF CAREER*

"*Design Your Life* is a wake-up call. It's the alarm clock you didn't know you needed, ringing loudly in the era of remote work and creator economy. Ignore at your own risk." PAUL SCHERER, CHIEF OF STAFF AT AUGMENT.ORG

"This book is a masterclass in finding your true calling. Erifili blends wisdom with practical steps, making it a must-read for Gen Z in particular to navigate their career with purpose and passion. Could not recommend more!" IDEJA BAJRA, FOUNDER AND CEO OF EDVANCE AI

"With *Design Your Life*, Erifili Gounari provides remarkable clarity and insights to Gen Zs on how to navigate the fast changing external environment and how to extract opportunities from the new digital world. Through the lens of her experience, she offers insights that will not only make digital entrepreneurship accessible to anyone but also enable Gen Zs to redefine what success means in a modern world. I highly recommend this book for prospective entrepreneurs and businesses keen to understand this new 'career' paradigm." LESLIE MAASDORP, VICE PRESIDENT AND CFO AT NEW DEVELOPMENT BANK (JULY 2015–JULY 2024)

"Erifili Gounari offers not only an inspirational look at the major challenges of digital natives, but also the very real opportunities they have to convert headwinds into propitious tailwinds. By applying the sum of her own peerless experience, she helps Gen Zs to shape their own future and to shape the future of the world. This book is a must read for Gen Z entrepreneurs and those who want to understand them." FRANK-JÜRGEN RICHTER, CHAIRMAN AND FOUNDER OF HORASIS AND FORMERLY DIRECTOR OF THE WORLD ECONOMIC FORUM

"Discover Gen Z's approach to side gigs, marketing and more in *Design Your Life*. Packed with novel insights and practical advice on personal branding and remote work, this book redefines success for a new generation. As a Gen Zer myself, I resonated deeply with many perspectives and, at the same time, took copious notes on how to (re-)design my own life now. A must-read for those eager to connect with Gen Z and thrive in today's fast-paced world. (My favourite tip: Get things done.)" KAI KRAUTTER, PHD IN ORGANIZATIONAL BEHAVIOUR AT HARVARD BUSINESS SCHOOL RESEARCHING PASSION FOR WORK

Design Your Life

Your career, your way

Erifili Gounari

KoganPage

Publisher's note
Every possible effort has been made to ensure that the information contained in this book is accurate at the time of going to press, and the publishers and authors cannot accept responsibility for any errors or omissions, however caused. No responsibility for loss or damage occasioned to any person acting, or refraining from action, as a result of the material in this publication can be accepted by the editor, the publisher or the author.

First published in Great Britain and the United States in 2025 by Kogan Page Limited

2nd Floor, 45 Gee Street
London
EC1V 3RS
United Kingdom
www.koganpage.com

8 W 38th Street, Suite 902
New York, NY 10018
USA

© Erifili Gounari 2025

ISBNs
Hardback   9781398617223
Paperback 9781398617155
Ebook   9781398617216

British Library Cataloguing-in-Publication Data
A CIP record for this book is available from the British Library.

Library of Congress Cataloging-in-Publication Data
Names: Gounari, Erifili, author.
Title: Design your life : your career, your way / Erifili Gounari.
Description: Second edition. | London ; New York, NY : Kogan Page, 2024. |
   Includes bibliographical references and index.
Identifiers: LCCN 2024026008 | ISBN 9781398617155 (paperback) | ISBN
   9781398617223 (hardback) | ISBN 9781398617216 (ebook)
Subjects: LCSH: Success in business. | Leadership.
Classification: LCC HF5386 .G62 2024 | DDC 650.1–dc23/eng/20240701
LC record available at https://lccn.loc.gov/2024026008

Typeset by Hong Kong FIVE Workshop
Print production managed by Jellyfish
Printed and bound by CPI Group (UK) Ltd, Croydon, CR0 4YY

Kogan Page books are printed on paper from sustainable forests.

CONTENTS

Acknowledgements

The process of writing this book has been the most rewarding experience. It is a vessel for everything I have learned so far about how you can work for yourself, create a fulfilling everyday life and make the absolute most of the tools and resources you have at your disposal, finding unconventional ways to create a life that makes you happy. Being able to share the lessons I've learned so far in a single piece of work gives me the opportunity to help anyone who might benefit from it, and that is a great privilege. So, thank *you* first and foremost, for trusting and reading this book. I'm very happy you're here!

There are a few people without whom this book wouldn't have been possible:

Thank you to Matt James and the Kogan Page team for making the book a reality, and being wonderful to work with at every step.

Thank you to every one of the incredible experts and entrepreneurs that contributed their time and insight to the book through interviews and conversations.

Thank you to every person on the Z Link team, for believing in my vision and contributing their talent and creativity to it each day.

Thank you to Maria and my Dad, for being my two first readers. I appreciate you, your feedback, your time and your support more than you know!

I am infinitely grateful to my parents, my sister and my closest loved ones – you know who you are and I appreciate you endlessly! Thank you for always supporting my writing, celebrating every little update with me, and being as excited about this book as I am. Your presence reminds me constantly that success is about creating space for the connections that matter.

Introduction

A few years ago, the idea that I could be leading a successful career in entrepreneurship and living my dream life in my early 20s seemed as distant as a trip to space. Yet, here I am, living proof that the careers and lives we dream of are not only possible but closer within reach than we tend to believe. I never had a plan for how my career would unfold: carrying a mix of skills and passions that didn't naturally fit together, I was never one of those people with a clear vision of how they would succeed. At university, I studied art history and digital media. I had no idea how I would use that, but I had to choose something, so I chose two fields that I felt drawn towards and decided that future me would figure out what my career would look like. Fast-forward to today: I am 24 years old, and have been the founder and CEO of The Z Link since I was 20. I started with no resources, no team, no investment and only basic entrepreneurship knowledge (free webinars, YouTube videos, you know how it is). Today, I lead an incredible global team of 25 ambitious Gen Zers, and we have been lucky enough to work with some of our favourite brands as clients, doing what we love. I had the privilege of being recognized on the *Forbes 30 Under 30* list in the Marketing and Youngest categories at the age of 23, as well as to travel around the world to speak at conferences and summits, meeting wonderful people at every turn. The best part? My job provides me with all the freedom I always assumed was unattainable at this age: full financial freedom so I can travel, treat my loved ones and feel comfortable, as well as tons of time and freedom to pursue passions and live a peaceful and fulfilling everyday life. If you are anything like me, you might think it sounds too good to be true. That is definitely what I used to think, until one thing led to the next.

When I was growing up, I had no idea that my career didn't have to be something I would dread, but could instead be something that would directly contribute to living my dream life. I was always taught that there were a couple of conventional paths I should aim to follow if I wanted security, stability and some version of success. When I chose to focus on literature and languages at school, I heard so many jokes about how that meant I'd end up with no job, making no money. Maybe I believed them to an extent, because no one told me otherwise. Everywhere around me, careers were viewed in the same way. Entrepreneurial education was not accessible or common, different types of self-employment were not encouraged and I thought I just had to choose between which industry my 9–5 office job would end up being in.

This is where I think careers education fails us. We have a long way to go in helping ambitious young people explore non-traditional career paths that could lead to much more fulfilling lives for them. This book unfolds from my unexpected journey, showing that no matter what success means to you, you can reach it with the right tools and actions. My work at The Z Link revolves around understanding Gen Z and helping the world connect with our generation. This means that I have conducted a lot of original research on Gen Z around the world, and have come to speak to hundreds of Gen Zers, seeing this pattern emerge too often: I speak to the most ambitious, skilled and driven people, often hearing 'I want to do something of my own but have no idea what or where to start.' The vast majority of friends stuck in corporate 9–5 jobs seem to want out, sensing that there is more for them out there, yet not knowing what steps to take to begin. They're not alone. These days, social media is full of videos and posts by people realizing that the traditional 9–5 career paths that they are expected to follow leave them feeling unfulfilled, drained of all energy and creativity, and with no free time.

We are seeing a surge of people exasperated at the impossibility of balancing everything: a 9–5 job, a social life, a good sleep schedule, healthy relationships, time to spend on passions and hobbies, and time to rest; they are seeking something better, a life where their career can contribute to their personal freedom. And that is completely reasonable: living a life where all of your energy and time is drained through work should not be the norm, not at a time when there are far better options available to us. Just because something has been done in a certain way for years, does not mean it is the best way to do it; and this is where a lot of generational miscommunications tend to occur. Our generation is pushing for a change in a work culture that has remained largely unchanged for over 100 years even as technology has advanced at great rates. We have the tools and technology to create better lives through more efficient and healthily productive careers, and we do not use them enough. Once we realize that this work culture is outdated, it is easy to understand why most Gen Zers want to learn how to work *smarter*, not harder, in order to create lives they love. Over 73 per cent of Gen Zers choose personal fulfilment and work-life balance as their top two priorities in choosing a career.[1] We are increasingly seeing experiments and research that prove that, by changing how we work, we can significantly improve our happiness and productivity. For example, companies that tested four-day work weeks while maintaining the same benefits and salary for their employees saw that productivity either remained the same or increased, with a large increase in happiness and decrease in stress and burnout.[2] We know there are better ways to work, the proof just keeps coming. But we don't need to wait for the world to catch up and start shifting – we can actively pursue alternative career paths that enable us to do just that: work smarter, be happier and overall feel better and more fulfilled.

This book is a practical guide for anyone in a similar situation, whether you're a student, a graduate or stuck in a job that you don't love. It offers insights and strategies to help you create a life you love in every way, supported by your career rather than hindered by it. It is a testament to the idea that the paths to our most ambitious goals are often less obstructed than we think, and I'm here to help you break down each doubt, obstacle and element of confusion stopping you from reaching your full potential. Some of the most impactful entrepreneurship books and career guides have become outdated due to the fast pace in which our world is evolving, as digital tools and the internet are opening up an entirely new world of opportunity for ambitious young people. This book offers advice from one digital native to another, because while generations aren't all that different to each other, Gen Z is the first to be able to benefit from this unprecedented field of opportunities. It's a shame to miss out and not use it to our advantage.

Digital tools and resources are invaluable for finding success in the modern world. I have seen this first-hand so often in my life. When I was 16, I learned that running an internet-based side gig could be fun and easy. I started a side gig making and selling bookmarks, and managed to get consistent sales by creating a small but engaged online community through social media that loved the products. Later on, I saw how my exposure to different types of content through years of browsing social media and the internet led to the idea for my company popping into my head, one quiet day during my third year of university.

Being a chronically curious person and having access to the internet proved to be an advantage: I had seen so many examples of people online following their own untraditional career paths and succeeding in ways I never knew were possible, so it slowly taught me that it could be an option for me too.

My own story went like this: I had been working office jobs alongside university to make a little money, doing the only thing I knew how to do well: social media marketing. The same pattern kept emerging in every job and team I joined. I was young, and they wanted someone young to help them connect with our generation through social media. I realized that there was a clear opportunity there: a Gen Z-led social media agency that would help brands connect with our generation in a way that actually resonated with us. It would later expand to also include market research, which now positions us as a leading source in helping brands and the world connect with Gen Z. Thus The Z Link was born. While I didn't know if it would succeed, I knew that all the resources I needed to experiment and find out if it *could* succeed were freely available at my fingertips. I had no savings, but my university studies and part-time job left me with some extra hours during which I decided to find out how to bootstrap a company and get it off the ground. I read classic books like *The Lean Startup*, learning to just put something out there, *anything*, instead of delaying it for months.

All parts of the journey were unconventional and didn't fit with what I had been taught a career would look like: getting my first few clients was a result of becoming good at personal branding on social media, and building a team was something I had to learn through trial and error. I found out that there were remote jobs that would allow you to work from anywhere and pay six figures for skills related to tech, growth and marketing, if you were experienced enough. That is how I funded my startup without ever raising investment, by stumbling upon one of these jobs that seem too good to be true, but actually exist thanks to the internet. I now see how useful it would have been to have had access to more of this knowledge throughout my own journey, and how a resource is needed that can guide young people towards using all the assets at their disposal to build careers they love and create personal freedom.

The aim of this book is to be as useful as possible. I want you to finish the book feeling like your version of success is attainable, and with a clear understanding of what steps you need to take to get there. It is actionable and practical, while also encouraging you to think about the big questions that will help you get to know yourself better, which are necessary in order to build a life you love. Through this book, you will learn how to harness the 'digital native advantage': the unique advantages we have thanks to being young at a time when the internet provides unprecedented opportunities. You will learn to deconstruct your definition of success and settle on what it means for you, so you can reach it: do you aim for complete freedom and flexibility in your daily life or for something more driven by societal impact and purpose? The questions around success are big ones, so we'll break them down in a way that helps you assess your priorities and envision the kind of life you want to live.

Then, we will get into the more practical side of things: side gigs, types of independent work, learning how to take the first steps whether you currently have a traditional job or not, along with insights from case studies and interviews with people who have carved their own paths to success. If you aim to work remotely or be a digital nomad, you will learn how to make that type of work successful and productive, as well as how to decide what type of work would best suit your personality and goals. Then, a full masterclass in personal branding: it has been my greatest asset while building my career, and drawing from my own journey in personal branding as well as my years of work in social media strategy, I will break down exactly how you can build a strong personal brand using social media. Your personal brand is what will work for you while you sleep, connecting you with opportunities and people thanks to how you position yourself, no matter what stage of your career you are in – even if you are a student with zero work experience.

In Chapter 6, which is almost like a mini-MBA, you will learn how to recognize whether a business idea is worth pursuing or an industry is worth investing your time and effort in: it discusses all you need to know about analysing and evaluating trends and opportunities, as well as providing specific tools, resources and strategies that you can experiment with. And finally, it is time to address all the usual fears and doubts that are likely holding you back, exploring how you can plan for the long term, face imposter syndrome, deal with failure and the fear of being judged, and push yourself to start *taking action*. We live in the very best time to create our own opportunities; we do not have to wait for the 'perfect' ones to land right in front of us. You can build a career on your terms, one that is centred around ownership, flexibility and freedom. Read on, and the prospect of building a career that directly leads to you living a life you love will go from being a distant and confusing goal to an actual plan.

Notes

1   The Z Link (2023) Gen Z + Careers, The Z Link, www.thezlink.com/research/careers (archived at https://perma.cc/7DKQ-ZC9V)
2   World Economic Forum (2023) Four-day work week trial in Spain leads to healthier workers, less pollution, www.weforum.org/lagenda/2023/10/surprising-benefits-four-day-week (archived at https://perma.cc/AYC2-WFX7)

CHAPTER ONE

The digital native advantage

Gen Z is the first generation of digital natives: having grown up with social media and the internet as an active part of our lives, we are the first generation to be shaped by digital technologies as part of our upbringing. Never knowing a world without the internet is at the core of the characteristics that differentiate Gen Z from earlier generations. It has heavily influenced our expectations regarding access to information, the content that we consume, the ways that we interact with people and the ways we want to be educated and entertained. Social media has become an indispensable part of our everyday lives. According to research conducted in 2022 in the United States, 38 per cent of Gen Z stated they used social media for four or more hours per day. Just four per cent of respondents said they used it for less than one hour daily, and two per cent reported they did not use social media at all.[1] When any technology becomes such an integral part of a cohort's life, it naturally leads to some shifts in behaviour, like low attention span and the tendency to gravitate towards instant gratification.

According to McKinsey's research on what differentiates Gen Z:

> digital natives often turn to the internet when looking for any kind of information, including news and reviews prior to making a purchase. They flit between sites, apps, and social media feeds, each one forming a different part of their online ecosystem. Having grown up with social media, Gen Zers curate their online selves more carefully than those in prior generations have, and they are more likely to turn to trends of anonymity, more personalized feeds, and a smaller online presence, even as they voraciously consume media online.[2]

Being digital natives has also led us to a culture of connectivity that transcends geography. Our generation's relationships and the communities in which we participate are increasingly facilitated by online channels, and it is common to value friends made online just as much as those made in person. One interesting consequence from this has been the fact that Gen Z is more attuned to other cultures and international events than generations before it, and it is also considered to be the most ethnically and racially diverse generation to date.[3] Yet, as expected, this constant connectedness has its challenges. The rise of influencer culture has not only changed our consumption patterns, by creating a whole new medium for lifestyle and product recommendations, but it has also shaped our career aspirations. A lot of Gen Zers now aim to carve a career path in content creation or digital entrepreneurship, with countless examples on their social media feeds daily showing them that it is possible. Content-based projects such as podcasts and blogs can become more than simple side gigs: they can be a livelihood and lucrative career. Emma Chamberlain, one of the most successful Gen Z content creators, launched her career through YouTube and Instagram by posting relatable content showing her real, authentic self. Today, she has managed to expand her career to include a podcast that ranked as one of Spotify's top five podcasts in 2023, as well as a successful self-named coffee brand. She is a prime example of how a regular Gen Z digital native can transform daily moments into content that resonates with others, and thus create a hyper-successful career by such a young age. Digital platforms have created an entirely new medium that we have come to consider a viable potential source of income and opportunity, and many of today's full-time jobs didn't exist a few years ago. However, an emerging pattern amidst these digital habits is a yearning for authenticity and genuine experiences, which platforms like BeReal are beginning to address, acknowledging Gen Z's desire to share unfiltered moments in a seemingly overly curated online world.

But above all, this trait has provided our generation with a competitive edge in many areas: that is the digital native advantage. This is something all Gen Zers should learn to embrace and cultivate in order to take full advantage of how these skills can help us steer our careers and lives in the right direction. Of course, any generation can implement the tips and tools covered in this chapter – everyone has the potential to use technology to transform their life for the better. But as Gen Z's intuitive fluency with technology positions us at the forefront of digital transformation, we have a head start in learning how to effectively harness this trait. If we also cultivate an understanding of digital trends and online consumer behaviour, we can navigate and innovate in ever-evolving landscapes like e-commerce, digital marketing and social media. Entrepreneurship can become a lot easier than it used to be because it is facilitated by the countless digital tools at our disposal – all we have to do is find them and learn to take advantage of them. A lot of Gen Zers do not recognize the innate skills that this digitally native upbringing has instilled in them: adaptability to new technologies can translate into an inclination towards problem-solving and critical thinking in digital contexts. And of course, the global communities we have access to on social media can facilitate unprecedented opportunities for learning, collaboration and networking. We can use that to influence and drive social change on a scale that previous generations could not access, simply because these technologies did not exist. This over-connectedness can therefore be an advantage. The digital proficiency of Gen Z is not just a generational trait, but a potent tool that we should be using to shape our personal and professional lives.

Sherry Ning, the 23-year-old writer of popular newsletter Pluripotent who has amassed over 80,000 followers on Twitter/X by sharing her writing and ideas, sees the ways in which being a digital native has given her an advantage in her career:

Being familiar with technology, popular software and social media definitely gives Gen Z an advantage. New platforms are easy to adjust to since every site basically shares the same format (e.g. 'post' button at the bottom, direct messages on the panel, etc). There is also an unspoken language – a culture – that comes with internet language; I don't just mean slang, I mean subtleties like what certain emoji reactions mean on an Instagram story (it can mean support, it can indicate someone's romantic interest in you, it can also just be used to get someone's attention). These subtle forms of non-written communications are typically the most difficult for non-digital natives to adjust to because it is so naturally embedded in internet culture.

Even in ways we do not think about or actively recognize, growing up as digital natives has equipped us with some skills that can be used to fuel our careers.

Careers and entrepreneurship

The way our generation thinks of careers has also been heavily influenced by this digitally native upbringing. Perhaps the biggest shift has been in how we regard entrepreneurship and innovation. Gen Z is a highly entre-preneurial generation, with 55 per cent of Gen Zers surveyed in 39 countries stating that they want to be self-employed or become entrepreneurs, rather than work for someone else, whether at a startup or large company.[4] It all comes back to access: entrepreneurship used to be inaccessible, risky and a rare path to follow. Today, we are exposed to so many alternative ways of working through social media that the entrepreneurial path has become normalized and a lot more accessible. The barrier to entrepreneurship is no longer as high. There are countless digital tools that we can use to build something even without coding, such as launching a simple landing page, and marketing a product or service. You no longer need a large budget to test out a digital-first product or service and determine whether it has product-market fit, which with some strategic social media marketing can then turn into a business. As Gen Z is growing up, the internet is evolving alongside us to make innovation increasingly easy and inclusive. With how quickly digital tools and new technologies are moving, we can only begin to imagine how easy creating something of your own will become in the coming years.

Another way Gen Z's views on careers tend to differ is through the access the internet has given us to healthier, more productive and fulfilling ways of working. Technology has enabled remote work to become a new norm, with 68 per cent of Gen Zers preferring hybrid work, and only six per cent favouring the office above remote or hybrid working.[5] We have seen how hybrid work can transform our lives, and spending hours commuting or killing time just because of set office hours no longer seems like a worthy compromise for most of us. A large proportion of Gen Z entered the workplace when remote work became prominent, so many of us have barely known a world where flexibility was not an option. When asked how important having the choice to work remotely is for them, only seven per cent of Gen Zers said that it is not important.[6] Along with the rise of remote work came the rise of digital nomad lifestyles, all leading back to the importance of flexibility and work-life balance, two traits that have become more important than ever to this generation. The rise of remote working and digital nomadism also means that we are increasingly relying on digital experiences and interactions for work, making the digital native advantage more valuable than ever. Combine this with Gen Z's entrepreneurial aspirations, and it's clear that autonomy and independence is hugely important. This is what building a career on our terms is about: through technology we have become accustomed to the possibility that work can be done better, that traditional paths have a lot of space for improvement.

Having observed the instability that often exists in traditional job markets and the rapid pace of change in the professional world, Gen Z has become more sceptical of traditional career paths. We are more likely to opt for a non-linear career and we are also more open to changing careers multiple times. Our views on careers as a whole have been determined by this digital native advantage – so how can we use it to break out of the mould and create value for ourselves, reach our goals and unlock new ways of working and living?

Harnessing the digital native advantage

Upskilling is easier than it ever was before. Any skill you want to learn is a couple of clicks away, for free. YouTube videos, articles and online courses exist to teach you pretty much *anything* you want to learn; that is perhaps one of the biggest advantages of being young while the internet exists. If you have some free time, as well as discipline, you can teach yourself dozens of skills that can directly allow you to build a career you love. As a digital native, picking up new technologies might come intuitively to you, depending on how involved you were with technology while growing up. This is something you should use to make your everyday life easier.

We practically live in an age that is a playground for the curious and the bold. The pursuit of knowledge and continuous experimentation are rewarded, and you can make a career out of experimenting with building products and solving problems. With discipline and consistency, the digital skills you can develop today can evolve into your dream career. The question isn't 'can you build your dream project?' – it's 'when will you start?'

Firstly, you can develop skills that allow you to *build*. If you learn to build your own products, you instantly unlock countless possibilities and directions your career could take. This is why SaaS (Software as a Service) startups are so popular. These days, starting your own business can be as simple as learning to build an app and understanding how to market it well. Of course there are so many parameters around that that can make or break your success, such as your network, your idea's product–market fit, your competition and a lot more, but the first stage is to understand that if you have ideas, you can learn to build them. Not only can you find hundreds of hours' worth of content teaching you to code, you can also learn to use no-code platforms that allow you to build apps with zero coding knowledge. For example, Bubble is a popular full-stack, no-code platform that allows you to design, develop and launch apps in a more intuitive way. A lot of impressive apps and online platforms have been built using no-code tools, such as Bloom Institute of Technology (formerly Lambda School), a platform that helps users launch their dream tech careers, or Outsite, a platform for remote workers to find communities to stay at around the world. AI has also been a game-changer in this field, with the rise of platforms that allow you to build apps in an even easier way, by using natural language that converts directly into the user interface of an app that you can preview live. All this information is freely available at your fingertips. The amount of tools that facilitate the development of these incredibly useful digital skills makes it harder to make any excuses – pretty much anything is possible. So, you have an idea for an app or product? Chances are you can find an online tool that will get you started in some way. It is only getting easier every day.

Ultimately, building products and coding is about creating solutions to problems people have. If you can understand user psychology and learn to make people's lives easier, you will be on the right track to creating successful digital products. Another essential area to look into, if this is something that interests you, is UX/UI (user experience and user interface) design. Understanding the fundamentals of UX/UI design will teach you to build human-centric products. The more intuitive and appealing they are, the more engaged and satisfied your users will be. All these skills are extremely useful, and if you are a digital native that can more easily pick up new tools, consider whether this is something that could align with your career goals.

Then comes marketing. It is easier than ever to learn how to market and sell through the internet. The best marketing knowledge is free. There are newsletters that break down exactly why a marketing strategy works or doesn't (my favourite ones are Rachel Karten's *Link in Bio*, and Harry Dry's *Marketing Examples*), and hundreds of creators out there dedicated to teaching you how to master social media marketing and content. Knowing how to market can transform your career, in many ways: marketing yourself (build a strong personal brand and it will work for you while you sleep), marketing a product you built or helping others market theirs. There are marketing courses available that are free, comprehensive and reputable, such as Google's Digital Garage, HubSpot's Ecommerce Marketing Training, Meta's courses on Facebook Blueprint and ads, Neil Patel's SEO courses, as well as many free courses on general digital and social media marketing offered by Udemy and FutureLearn. Great products fail all the time because of weak marketing.

Knowing how to sell is essential. It will serve you well regardless of your career path; it is a vital skill for job interviews and it's also essential for selling a product or service. The amount of free resources out there is endless. Start with digital marketing and SEO, and you are already opening new doors for yourself. You might have heard the saying 'attention is currency'. Learning to market and sell online is how you capture that attention. Social media marketing also naturally tends to come more easily to Gen Z than older generations. When I worked in social media marketing before I started my own company, the brands I worked with always emphasized how they wanted to hire a young marketer who easily understood social media, so even with only a couple of years of experience under my belt at that point, I would get hired. That's because underneath those official years of experience were the years I spent between the ages of 11 and 16 just playing around with social media as a fun hobby, posting about my passions and interests, and creating communities that eventually turned into pages with tens of thousands of followers across platforms. This is a Gen Z experience (and now, Gen Alpha). A lot of us acquired digital skills that are now entire careers just by growing up playing around with technology. When it comes to marketing, creating multi-channel campaigns requires a deep understanding of each platform's subtleties, trends, what works and what doesn't. As a Gen Zer, you likely have a lot of that innate understanding already, by using these platforms as part of your daily life – a lot of these subtleties cannot be easily taught or explained, because they tend to be quite subconscious. Of course, this is not the case for everyone; no generation is a monolith and there are exceptions to everything. But research shows us that the majority of Gen Zers share a lot of these common points.

Beyond social media marketing, there is social media literacy. It is an increasingly important skill that translates into networking, personal branding and information literacy. Accustoming yourself to reaching out to people on social media and becoming comfortable with posting content online, if you are not already, is almost essential for any ambitious Gen Zer. Even if you are not a marketer, these skills can push your career forward more than you can imagine. This is something we will explore in-depth in Chapter 5, Personal branding. It is natural for our generation to connect with anyone we might want to collaborate with on social media, to broaden our network and to access opportunities this way. Creating a first-class job application is no longer the only way to secure that dream job; you could also land it by networking. There are so many new ways to access opportunities and build a career that you will not find in a traditional career guide, so embracing the digital native advantage is crucial.

Online networking is a skill like any other – you can learn to go out there and create life-changing connections instead of waiting for it to happen by itself. While building your personal brand will increase the likelihood of the right people coming *to* you, there are many things you can do to be proactive with online networking as well. A couple of decades ago, reaching out to an industry expert, business leader or potential mentor was a complicated process, even if they lived in your city. If they were in another country, that was an even more impossible feat. Today you can just reach out to them on social media. The process has been fully normalized and access has become universal; you just need a social media profile. You can take a methodical approach to online networking: make a list of people you want to connect with, even if you don't know the person themselves (for example, your list might include 'Head of Marketing at [Company]'). Think of people you could learn something from, collaborate with in some way or those who have the career you aspire to. Then, do your research and find them on a platform like LinkedIn. Connect with them and reach out if you have something kind or thoughtful to say, but keep online networking etiquette in mind: no one likes to receive messages just asking them for things, especially if they are in a position where they get those kinds of messages all the time. You can also join groups and communities built specifically for online networking. LinkedIn itself has groups you can join related to different topics and industries, and you can also find dozens of active communities hosted on platforms like Slack, Discord and Circle. If you are not already a member, it is time to do some research and find active communities in your field of interest. Some of them are free and some are paid, but there is something for everyone. Being intentional about building your network using online tools is an indispensable career skill. Through online communities, I have met people that ended up becoming clients for my marketing agency, made friends and also networked with experts that taught me how to advance my business. There is a community for almost everything out there, but if you don't find what you are looking for, that is good too – it just means you can start one yourself!

While we will explore side gigs in detail in Chapter 3, it is worth mentioning that another way to use the digital native trait to your advantage is by exploring the platforms available to you for freelance work and for easy ways to get side jobs, if you are unsure about what you want to work on. Platforms like Upwork, Fiverr and Contra are very easy to use for anyone familiar with digital platforms and social media: all you have to do is build a profile based on your skills and the types of services you can offer, and start submitting proposals to relevant jobs or receiving requests from those hiring. It is becoming increasingly common for Gen Zers to take on freelance work alongside their studies, as there are truly so many services you can offer that are in demand. If you speak multiple languages, you can learn to offer translation services. If you code, you can offer web development or software services. If you are learning marketing, sales or SEO, you will see hundreds of jobs posted daily looking for freelancers to help with these areas. These are usually international so it does not matter where you are based. One of the best things about the popularity of freelance platforms is how inclusive they are to anyone, regardless of experience or location. Through such platforms, it is easy to build a portfolio for skills you want to focus your career around. You can take small projects alongside your studies or your main job, and start building proof of work around an area that you are passionate about. Whether you do it to build a portfolio, to earn some extra money or to figure out what you like and don't like doing, freelancing should be quite intuitive as a Gen Zer. You can learn all the skills you need online, and then start offering them to those who need them.

This would not be a complete chapter on the digital native advantage without referring to artificial intelligence. If you are a Gen Zer, you are lucky to be growing up at a time when AI progress is happening rapidly. Whether we are ready to accept it or not, as Gen Zers, AI will be a part of our life in some way as we grow. Even if you are more of a sceptic on the topic, the great thing is that you can use AI tools in so many ways to facilitate your everyday life, which a year ago would have been unimaginable. New AI tools are emerging every single day to create unprecedented possibilities to enhance productivity, creativity and innovation. Generative language models like ChatGPT can be used as personal assistants to aid with data gathering and analysis, brainstorming, conducting research, helping you organize and structure ideas, deconstructing opportunities and problems, and even helping with decision-making. When it comes to careers, you can use AI to expand on entrepreneurial ideas, develop detailed plans for new ventures, or analyse a career move you are considering. You basically have the world's knowledge at your fingertips, and AI tools make that more manageable and easily accessible, so you can spend more time thinking about what matters, and less time sorting through infinite information. They can analyse job market trends, helping you identify skills that are in demand and industries that are on the rise. They can help you create personalized learning plans to develop your skills, tailored to your learning preferences and interests, so that you can have a more rewarding learning experience.

AI tools that deconstruct and prioritize tasks can help you become more productive, drawing insight from your work habits, optimizing your time and planning your day according to your own work patterns. Instead of dampening creativity or taking away from creative industries, AI tools can act as a catalyst for creativity instead, by facilitating brainstorming, new perspectives, getting you out of creative blocks and automating the more routine parts of creative work. This is a very fast-moving area, with new developments happening every day. It is important to keep an eye open for new releases that could supercharge your productivity; but regardless of platform or application, the core remains true: if you approach AI from a perspective of making it work alongside you to enhance your capabilities and open more doors, the possibilities are endless, and they are only increasing every day.

Making the mindset shift

Above all else, the internet introduces new avenues to what is possible. Side projects like a freelance job, social media page or a newsletter can become full-time entrepreneurial ventures. A big part of using the digital native advantage to its full potential is making the necessary mindset shift from what you think and have been told is possible to what actually is. If your goal is financial freedom or a job you love and are excited about, you have to think outside the box. Don't look at what everyone in your circle is doing unless you want to do the same thing. This mindset shift is essential, and it has to happen consciously. In order to develop new skills and use all the technologies and tools available at your fingertips, you have to actually believe that you can learn anything you want – that is a growth mindset, and more often than not we have been taught not to have it.

A growth mindset is one where you believe you can learn anything you want with practice, which is absolutely the case. A fixed mindset, on the contrary, sees skills and traits as fixed and believes you should not waste your time trying to acquire new traits you might not already feel like a natural at. In *Mindset: The new psychology of success*, Carol Dweck writes 'The passion for stretching yourself and sticking to it, even (or especially) when it's not going well, is the hallmark of the growth mindset.' In my opinion, there has never been a better time to have a growth mindset. Many of the common objections to developing any skill you want and learning new things have basically been overthrown by the current access we have to information. What do you feel is holding you back because you are not good at it right now? If you keep referring back to one thing (e.g. 'I'd start something of my own but I'm not technical/I don't know anything about entrepreneurship/I have no idea how to sell a product'), you need to take a close look at it and ask yourself whether you are using it as an easy excuse to not take the leap. Yes, when you try something new, you can fail. But failure is an opportunity, and seeing it as such, even when the experience is painful, is a key trait of the growth mindset. Dweck also writes: 'When they [NASA] were soliciting applications for astronauts, they rejected people with pure histories of success and instead selected people who had had significant failures and bounced back from them.' When you fail, you learn, and learning is invaluable. In other words, it is impossible to build your dream career and life without ever failing at anything – that would mean you never took a leap or a risk, and how much can be achieved without that?

Therefore, acknowledge the special privilege of having been born at a time of such access and information, and recognize that the digital world is there for you to take advantage of. If that still feels unattainable, it is a sign that you might have to actively work on shifting your mindset as you go. Shifting your mindset is not a one-off project, but a continuous effort. I first realized my mindset was holding me back when I was around 16 or 17 years old, and decided to start doing a lot of research on how to improve it. I realized my negative thinking patterns were destructive. I learned to catch negative thoughts and shift them to positive ones, to recognize when I was holding myself back by making excuses or judging myself, instead of believing in all the possibilities that were available to me, and in my own capacity to take advantage of them. Since then, I have understood how crucial maintaining a healthy mindset is in order to achieve my goals. It has been vital in the success of my business and in my ability to embark on new initiatives. We tend to be really bad at accurately estimating our abilities, and our instinct more often than not will be to underestimate what we can learn and how far we can go. But the truth is that we can learn anything. In a few years, your skillset and strengths can be completely different to what they are right now. You are not in any way constrained by what you are good at today – that is not a box you have to stay within.

Alongside skill-building, you can use the internet as a tool to find opportunities and spot trends early on. As a digital native, spotting promising opportunities can become second nature if you learn to look. Why would you want that? Because being able to spot trends and hop on them early, and using good judgement to decipher when it is worth it and when it is not, can lead to new avenues for success that others might easily miss. Firstly, there are newsletters you can subscribe to and online communities you can join that specialize in exactly this. One such community is *Trends* by The Hustle: they send a weekly

newsletter that spots early trends that are on the rise, identifying relevant business opportunities and showcasing the
data to support them. They can range from areas like
consumer goods, to healthcare, to anything else at all that
they deem insightful. They do all the research for you, and
report back with interesting opportunities and insights.
The internet is full of creators and platforms dedicated to
bringing you value in some way; it is just about finding the
right ones and using them to think outside the box. If you
follow the right people on platforms like Twitter/X, you
can get similar value for free: hundreds of creators out
there are committed to spotting interesting trends and
sharing opportunities, but you can't expect them to just
come to you. You have to be proactive about curating your
social media feed or your email inbox with content that is
also valuable in addition to the content you consume for
entertainment. Once you become intentional about the
content you consume and you realize that you can curate
it in a way that works in your favour, then new opportunities will literally appear in front of you as you scroll. Soon
enough, you will also start to notice trends pop up yourself. For example, most of the people I follow on Twitter/X
are part of the tech startup ecosystem. So, when I notice
that I have been seeing a topic appear a bit more often
than usual on my feed, and people are talking about it
more, it is a good sign that it is an area to watch. You
develop your own radar for identifying opportunities just
by recognizing patterns. If you spend time scrolling on
social media already anyway, why not make it work a little
harder for you? Gen Z gets so many unhealthy side-effects
from using social media so actively, but opportunities arise

when we figure out how to turn that around and transform it into a space of value, inspiration and knowledge.

The unhealthy side-effects of social media and the internet are the main components of the digital native *disadvantage*, which are important to acknowledge. Researchers have suggested that the increasing use of social media among young people is generating higher levels of anxiety and depression among this generation.[7] And it is not surprising – with the rise of influencer culture highlighting the world's most perfectly curated collection of everyday moments, anyone exposed to that type of content often enough is bound to start comparing themselves with others. Social media showcases the best of people's personal and professional lives, and seeing that during Gen Z's most formative years naturally contributes to anxiety around whether they are doing enough or whether they will be successful 'early enough'. The positive side of this is that it has created a wave of a lot more real content all over social media, aiming to showcase people and stories that are more human, and less perfect. To mitigate that anxiety, especially if you are someone who works online a lot, it is essential to stick to some mindfulness habits to remain balanced. My favourite ones are journaling and meditating every day. Writing regularly in a journal is incredibly underrated as a tool to process your emotions and daily life, and to get to understand yourself better. It is by far the most rewarding habit I have chosen to stick to in my life, and one of those things I believe everyone should be doing. Through all the time we spend using technology, we tend to stem further away from that – writing can help us get closer again, so our brains get some time to actually slow down and process.

When it comes to meditating, it is also an effective tool to counterbalance our largely digital lives. Ironically enough, the best way to start incorporating meditation into your daily routine is through online apps; my favourite one is *Insight Timer*. There are a lot of great apps focused on digital wellness that you can integrate in your life to regain your peace of mind among the noise. I recommend *One Sec*, an app that delays the opening of any social media app you choose, and instead prompts you to take a breath for a few seconds and become present again. All of our lives are affected to some degree by growing up alongside social media and the internet, so spending some time to find the habits and tools that will help us become more mindful and stay present is essential for a happy life in the long term.

Creating your digital ecosystem

The digital native advantage can help you become a more organized, productive and creative version of yourself. Technology can work in your favour to help you reach your goals and build your career more efficiently. When it comes to productivity, there has never been a better time to be born. We get to shape our careers at a time where we can use technology to generate so much potential. Think of the way you use technology as a customized digital ecosystem that you can build to make your life better. It includes everything mentioned above, the ways you curate your social media feeds, the communities you are a member of, the newsletters you subscribe to and more. It also includes the tools you put in place to use every day for specific functions. Supporting and facilitating productivity can be one of those functions. The goal is to create a digital ecosystem that supports your own personal productivity rhythm. What works for your favourite productivity influencer might not necessarily work for you, so experiment, try out a few different things and see what helps you become your best and most productive version. There are countless tools out there to cater to different needs. Personally, my productivity ecosystem is quite simple (and for all I know, might change in a couple of months). Here is what I currently use:

- Microsoft To Do: To track daily tasks, because it has only the basic features needed with no extra noise, and it syncs immediately between devices.
- *Notion*: To track my yearly goals, personal and professional projects, and to keep track of interesting links I stumble upon that I want to save for future reference.
- *One Sec* app: To block access to social media apps when I want to stay focused.
- Apple *Notes*: Used for literally everything else, such as daily ideas, quick notes and thoughts I want to deal with later.
- Apple's *Reminders and Calendar* apps: I am all about simplicity, so I use these two default Apple apps, because unless I feel like something is missing, I would rather not add tools with tons of extra features to my daily life.

- Superhuman: Probably the most non-essential but extremely useful tool that I use every day. I send tons of emails as part of my work, and Superhuman is an email client that organizes my emails and allows me to do everything considerably faster, saving me a lot of time and automating many tedious email processes.

Of all those, Apple *Notes* is probably the one I could not live without, because it has become an extension of my brain. Having a space to collect scattered thoughts and ideas helps me tremendously; I do not have to worry about forgetting things or having to deal with something *right now*, and that allows me to focus, clear my mind and remain productive. This is just the system that works for me, but the ideal one for you would likely be different. There are great apps like *Evernote* that can serve the same purpose as *Notion* or Apple *Notes*, it is just a matter of finding what you feel more natural working with. This is a pursuit worth spending some time on, to ensure you can create a digital ecosystem that is tailored to the ways *you* work best. If you struggle to focus and are prone to distractions, you could try apps like *Forest*, built specifically to help you stay focused by keeping you off your phone. If you can identify your weaknesses or the traits that prevent you from reaching your full potential day to day, you can most likely find solutions to them through technology.

At the end of the day, building a useful digital ecosystem is about freeing up your time and clearing your mind so you can focus on strategic or creative thinking. A lot of the tasks we waste hours on every year can be automated. If you are working on your personal brand or creating regular social media content, you should be scheduling social media posts using tools like Buffer or Metricool. If you have to send a lot of emails like me, maybe you want to consider investing in a tool like Superhuman so that you can streamline the process as much as possible, create reusable email templates or speed up everything through shortcuts. If you are more tech-savvy and interested in automating your daily tasks even more, then tools like Zapier could be for you, where you can create hundreds of different automations by integrating tools in any way you can imagine. Just remember that it is not about overcomplicating your life by using every digital resource you can find, but about finding ways to use technology to gain time freedom, focus and mental clarity: things that will directly contribute to you building your ideal career and life.

So whether you are Gen Z or older, it's vital that you draw upon the skills and insights behind the digital native advantage. It's something to lean on and embrace as an ambitious individual in order to unlock new opportunities and paths that your life and career could take. I would not be where I am today without social media, online communities and digital networking, nor can I imagine a world without all of these useful tools. If you are looking to build a career on your terms, technology will inevitably play a big role in facilitating that. You can learn any skill you want, connect with anyone around the world, test products and ideas, build and join communities, take advantage of AI and get inspired by the countless people out there sharing stories of their own alternative career paths on the internet. Whether your goal is more focused on personal success or on igniting societal change through your career, it is worth spending some time to find the tools and resources that can directly take you one step closer to achieving that.

Notes

1   Dixon, S J (2022) U.S. Gen Z daily time spent on socials, Statista. www.statista.com/statistics/1385608/us-gen-z-daily-time-spent-on-socials (archived at perma.cc/5THT-JY9Q)

2   McKinsey & Company (2023) What is Gen Z? www.mckinsey.com/featured-insights/mckinsey-explainers/what-is-gen-z (archived at perma.cc/FQV4-4JAY)

3   Parker, K and Igielnik, R (2020) On the cusp of adulthood and facing an uncertain future: What we know about Gen Z so far, Pew Research Center. www.pewresearch.org/social-trends/2020/05/14/on-the-cusp-of-adulthood-and-facing-an-uncertain-future-what-we-know-about-gen-z-so-far-2 (archived at perma.cc/47GG-6UDM)

4   The Z Link (2023) Gen Z + Careers. www.thezlink.com/research/careers (archived at perma.cc/7DKQ-ZC9V)

5   Ibid.

6   Ibid.

7   Twenge, J M (2017) Have smartphones destroyed a generation? The Atlantic. www.theatlantic.com/magazine/archive/2017/09/have-smartphones-destroyed-a-generation/534198/ (archived at perma.cc/94HZ-RN4X)

CHAPTER TWO

Redefining success

Designing a career on your terms is something completely personal. So, for this to work, you have to do some internal exploring to figure out what works for you: how you prefer to spend your days, what gives you energy, what drains you and, most importantly, what success looks like to you. Looking to other people for these answers won't help you guide your career decisions because they will not be aligned with your goals and values. Everyone has their own personal definition of success, but our upbringing and outside influences often restrict us from fully exploring our personal ambitions. Instead, life often presents us with a predefined mould of what a career and life trajectory should look like and teaches us to fit within it. But breaking out of this mould is possible, and more accessible than ever before. And we know that doing so is a lot more likely to result in a life that is fulfilling, and a career that actively contributes to a satisfying life.

Chances are you are reading this book because your current work situation is not entirely fulfilling – it might even be draining and negatively affecting your life. You might be stuck in a job you do not like which causes you constant stress, or you might still be a student that knows there are more possibilities out there beyond the traditional career pathways. Or you might simply have reached a point in your career where you feel like it is time for a change, on your terms, to get more out of life. Contrary to what many people put up with, work does not have to be something inherently stressful, or a burden to be dealt with as a default cost of being alive. Ideally, work should contribute to your fulfilment and happiness. Instead of being only a way to make ends meet, it can become a way to achieve what you see as a successful life. Whatever your situation is, the first step is to envision what success would look like to you. No one else's definition of success has any impact on whether you have 'made it' or not, as long as you feel like you have. It is essential to let go of all the external factors we use to define success and look internally.

Your own definition of success can stem from your background, your passions, your values, your aspirations or a combination of the above. The most common definitions of success that we tend not to question include making a lot of money, rising to a high position at a notable company or becoming a hyper-successful entrepreneur. But as we see time and time again, these types of success often fail to equate with happiness or fulfilment. What is the point of aiming to rise to the highest corporate position if it requires you spending the best years of your life working and stressing 24/7 to get there, justifying it as okay because you will enjoy life when you retire? What if we regarded success more as something that can be achieved in different ways throughout our life? It also depends on where you live: some countries are more traditional, seeing only traditional professions like medicine or law as true success, while others are more encouraging of entrepreneurship and innovation-based jobs. When it comes to individuals, definitions of success tend to vary drastically as well: some define it as working on something that improves society, managing to have a large and tangible social impact, driven by purpose. The goal for many is to make history in some way, with a focus on creating something that lasts. While to others, success means working as little as possible, so they can have the freedom and flexibility to live outside of work. All of these goals are valid.

There are two main branches dealing with the notion of purpose: some people aim to fulfil their purpose through their work while others aim to find the most efficient and easy way to sustain themselves so that they can explore and fulfil their purpose outside of work. I constantly see young ambitious people around me stress over finding their purpose. It is a question they keep pondering without knowing how to find the answer. Purpose is about contributing to something greater than oneself, finding a sense of higher meaning in our work. However, we rarely stop to question why we believe so strongly that purpose and work are tied together. They are for many people, but they do not have to be. It is important to actively expand our frame of thinking about work, purpose and success, to explore these big questions. The meaning in your work can simply be that it allows you to explore things you are passionate about outside of work, by giving you financial freedom and control over your time. It is also essential to understand that your definition of success and your sense of purpose will likely change over time as you change and grow. So pursuing a career path that gives you flexibility to adapt to your changing purpose and interests is valuable.

It's okay if you don't have the answer right now. So, how do you figure out where you stand? I am a big proponent of journaling, writing down everything on paper. Journaling helps you think better, because it forces you to slow down and become a more structured thinker. In a survey of people who journal regularly, 88 per cent of them reported that journaling helped them focus, 77 per cent stated that it helped them achieve their goals and 65 per cent stated it helped them manage stress, among many other benefits. Some 77 per cent also said that journaling helped them with self-discovery, namely understanding their beliefs, values and feelings about life.[1] So, take some time to put pen to paper and answer these questions, and see what comes up:

1 When have I felt most fulfilled? What was the reason?
2 What activities fill me with energy and make me lose track of time?
3 Do I feel like I need to find 'my purpose'? Do I already know what it is?

4 Do I believe that my work has to have some higher meaning?
5 What do I value more: contributing positively to society or my own personal happiness?
6 Would I be happy living a fully fulfilling life without making any big societal contributions or is that an essential aspect to reaching fulfilment for me?
7 What does a day in my dream life look like?

These questions should help you uncover what resonates most with you at this phase of your life. There are no right or wrong answers, nor should you judge yourself if your answers gravitate more towards personal happiness than altruism – the most important thing is to be completely honest in your answers, so that you can craft a career that leads you towards the most fulfilling life for you. It is also not a black and white type of problem; it is more like a spectrum, as many people fall somewhere in between for many of these questions.

A lot of the notions we hold around success are ones we have to unlearn. For example, would you rather make 10 times your current income in a stressful job that leaves you no free time or make enough money to live a comfortable life but with all the freedom and peace of mind of a fulfilling life? It is easy to gravitate towards choosing the options in which you make more and more money, but the goal is to find or create the options that offer both financial freedom and time freedom. Having only one without the other does not result in a fulfilling life. Financial freedom takes care of all the money-related anxieties which, even though they say money cannot buy happiness, can still result in a whole lot of unhappiness when there is a lack of it. The next level of financial freedom allows you to pursue your passions and explore life a lot more freely: travelling the world, treating the people you love, living in a place you love. But for that to happen, time freedom is essential. To me, the main measure of success is the ability to control your time, to have freedom over what you get to do. Being able to act upon my inspiration when it is sparked is very important to me. Whatever it may be – writing something, exploring an idea, jumping on a new hobby or reading a book – being able to pursue it when I feel most inspired brings a real sense of fulfilment to my daily life. I feel most fulfilled and engaged when I am able to spend time on what I deeply feel like spending time on at that moment. That realization has made me more intentional about inspiration: exposing myself to things that inspire me, noticing when I feel that sense of engagement and acting upon it when I have it. It is also how I get a lot of things done – because when I feel inspired by an idea or project, I act on it immediately, rather than waiting and letting my enthusiasm and momentum eventually die out. As a result, even if I got a job opportunity that offered a higher degree of some other factor (e.g. financial), I would probably still choose a lifestyle that has a higher degree of freedom while still providing me with a financial stability level that I am happy with.

For this chapter, I spoke to fellow Gen Z entrepreneurs and changemakers working across a variety of different disciplines around the world. I wanted to explore how our generation views success and what we are aiming to achieve in the coming years. Dominic Monn, the

26-year-old founder and CEO of global mentoring platform MentorCruise, sees success as a mix of the following factors: purpose, financial freedom, location independence and control over your time. 'So many dream of a fully passive income and then to sit on the beach all day. I don't think this is the path to happiness. When you combine both [purpose and freedom], you're working on something that matters, but it doesn't keep you from taking time off, exploring other interests, being healthy.' For Dominic, success is a combination of knowing that your work has some meaning or positive impact, but without that taking a toll on your own freedom and personal fulfilment. This is a pattern: you do not want your work to be an obstacle between you and your dream life, but rather a catalyst to accessing that. Taking time off, exploring passions and interests, and having the time to maintain healthy habits are all essential factors to a happy life. For many people, therefore, having a career that allows them to access all of the above translates into success. So, is success about achieving true work-life balance?

Sherry Ning, the 23-year-old prolific online writer of Pluripotent, explained to me that she sees work-life balance as absurd. Her personal view on success is that, at any given moment, she is always working and not working at the same time. 'Work and life should never be separate, what you do should align with who you are, and who you are should feed into, or accelerate, what you do.' So while some people crave work-life balance and a separation of the two (like a traditional 9–5 career), others like Sherry prefer for work and life to be inherently united. Where do you stand? If one side or the other instinctively resonates with you, then you can use that to inform the way you structure your career. If you want your work and life to be combined, find a career that you are passionate about, so that you can be content with defining yourself by your career and committing most of your time to it. On the other hand, if you'd prefer your professional and personal lives to be separated, then perhaps passion is less important than finding a job that you enjoy and that is financially rewarding, as you'll have more spare time to pursue your passions.

Understanding where you stand on this spectrum will give you the clarity needed in order to find the type of career that would work best for you. Another emerging pattern is that for many ambitious people, it all goes back to *ownership*. Ownership over your time, your work, the way you get to live. We are shifting increasingly towards an economy of ownership. It represents a shift in how the younger generations view their professional and personal lives. Rather than simply assuming roles within predefined structures, they are prioritizing control and autonomy. It is about being able to define the direction of your work and life, having a greater say in that narrative. This focus on ownership and control is inherently tied to fulfilment, which is very difficult to achieve within the bounds of a predefined and set structure.

Twenty-five-year-old Saish Rane is the co-founder and Managing Partner of Edenia Capital, a first-check investment fund focused on early-stage European climate-tech startups. His business was born out of a desire to create a way to support entrepreneurs coming out of school, and back ambitious founders that could build companies with great positive impact. For Saish, success is focused mainly on impact, and on ensuring that he takes advantage of every resource at his disposal to create positive change. 'Success to me is having used everything at my disposal, be it capital, knowledge, relationships, network, to further the cause of living in a better world.' If you feel the same way as Saish, then that is a sign that you need a career that provides you with the chance to work on something you consider impactful to society. Finding a career that checks all of your boxes is no easy feat, and that is why you need to reframe your thinking to go from just 'finding opportunities' to 'creating opportunities'. Creating opportunities can mean a lot of things: it could stem from founding your own company, community or organization, to reaching out to the right person at a company you want to work for that is not openly hiring, and explaining how you could help them by joining their team. What is certain is that crafting your ideal career is nearly impossible if you limit your opportunities just to job advertisements. You need to consider the opportunities beyond what you will find on job platforms, and think outside the box to either create or find the right openings for you, based on your strengths, goals and preferences.

Work preferences are also a key element to explore when understanding your personal definition of success. Figuring out what working style suits you best is essential. Traditional working styles that include working in an office from 9 to 5 or longer are not designed to make everyone their most productive self. While some people are indeed more productive in a structured office setting, others thrive when they can control more aspects of their day and their environment, leading to higher productivity at home. Others find inspiration from and are able to be productive while travelling and regularly changing scenery, while some prefer an intermediate solution such as working at cafes or co-working spaces. The latter is great for those who perform best when they have the flexibility of choice found in remote work, combined with the community elements found in going to an external environment to work with people around. Since the Covid-19 pandemic, there has been more than enough research conducted on the effects of remote work – so much so that we have ended up with a lot of conflicting data, creating further confusion for both companies and people about the future of work. For example, a study by Texas A&M University found that remote work does not lower productivity, while a study by Stanford's Institute for Economic Policy and Research found that remote work can decrease productivity by 10–20 per cent.[2,3] Whatever thesis you want to prove regarding remote work and productivity, you will find the statistics to support it. There is enough out there to convince you that remote work destroys productivity and also enough to show that people have never been more productive than when allowed to work remotely. But you do not need statistics to decide how and when you feel most productive. By now, we know better than to believe that any dogmatic stance on remote work is an absolute truth. Productivity is completely personal, and depends on how you work and feel best. Where it makes sense for the industry and the work, companies should always offer the option of remote or hybrid work. When everyone is able to work how they work best, they will be happier, more productive and more fulfilled, so flexibility is key.

Do you work best alone, at home or at a cafe? Do you enjoy being in an office setting or does it make no difference to you? Do you feel the need to travel often to stay inspired and productive or does traveling make it difficult for you to stick to any routine? Do you value socializing with colleagues in the office? Most of the Gen Z entrepreneurs I spoke to for this chapter mentioned the importance to their productivity and happiness of being able to take a walk or take a break to cook or exercise. The consistency of daily routines allows many people to thrive, as long as the routine is on their terms. Dominic Monn also mentions:

> I've found that I don't particularly enjoy nomadis. I do take workcations, where I may spend two–four weeks in a different city, but it's also clear to me that my overall productivity will drop. I think a routine works best for me, having a home base with a nearby gym and amenities. That being said, I've really enjoyed the flexibility to go visit a different country, as long as I have my laptop with me.

When you start having a career that allows you the flexibility to explore, experimenting with all these ways of working can provide useful insight into how you should craft your career as you grow. It is difficult to learn what works for you if you do not try it, and the things you find may often be unexpected. You might be drawn to a nomadic lifestyle only to try it and find that it distracts you too much, or you might indeed discover that it opens up new horizons for you and allows you to live your dream everyday life. Remember that this has nothing to do with what everyone else around you is doing – it is personal to you, and that is where your focus should be when exploring these questions. Just because people around you believe everyone is more productive in-office does not mean it is applicable to you too; similarly, being surrounded by happy remote workers and digital nomads does not mean it is the best way for you to work.

The role of failure

We cannot explore success without talking about failure. One of the main factors stopping people from taking a leap and pursuing their ambitions is a fear of failure, which is completely natural and something everyone deals with. It is a consequence of the way most people are raised – an overemphasis on intelligence and achievements which leads children, during their formative years, to believe that anything less than that is a failure. In *Mindset: The new psychology of success*, Carol Dweck has done some great work in explaining how most people view failure. She explains the correlation of praise with confidence, and consequently the development of an unhealthy relation-ship with making mistakes:

> After seven experiments with hundreds of children, we had some of the clearest findings I've ever seen: Praising children's intelligence harms their motivation and it harms their performance. How can that be? Don't children love to be praised? Yes, children love praise. And they especially love to be praised for their intelligence and talent. It really does give them a boost, a special glow—but only for the moment. The minute they hit a snag, their confidence goes out the window and their motivation hits rock bottom. If success means they're smart, then failure means they're dumb.[4]

This gets internalized to such a deep level that it becomes very hard to overcome as an adult. People that grew up being praised for their intelligence as a measure of success are likely to struggle even more with facing potential failures, because 'succeeding' has become part of their identity. They become perfectionists, and perfectionism is a trap. It goes back to the fixed mindset mentioned in the previous chapter.

Those with a fixed mindset value the outcome a lot more than the process, and therefore view the outcome as either a success or a failure. Those with a growth mindset, on the other hand, understand that the process is just as essential as the outcome, and that success and failure are not black and white. No attempt to create something or pursue your ambition is ever wasted, if you learn from the mistakes you make. As Malcolm Forbes said, 'Failure is success if we learn from it.'[5] When you fail, analyse the factors that led to it, and understand how valuable an opportunity it is to be able to learn from first-hand experience. Most importantly, know that failure is not personal, and taking it personally or thinking it defines you is bound to set you back and create anxieties and doubts that will plague your future efforts. Instead of making excuses or trying to blame failure on something, people with a growth mindset see failure as just an indicator that they should re-evaluate their strategy or apply more effort.

Most people think success is more about practical skills than mindset, but the truth is that mindset is where a substantial difference is made. Dweck's book shows that even in skill-based pursuits such as sports, teams that intentionally recruit athletes that have cultivated a growth mindset rather than only having the practical skills, see significant success because of it.[6] So success is also about being able to remain optimistic and have faith that you really can succeed; if you think you can't, research shows that you probably won't. A study of over 1,000 students found that optimistic people are genuinely more likely to succeed, especially when it is steady optimism that does not get knocked down over time.[7] Mindset is inherently tied into discussions around success, so it is worth taking a moment to consider whether you are happy with the way you currently think about these things or whether it might be beneficial to make an effort to shift your mindset more towards optimism, and examine your relationship with failure.

However, there is a big truth we need to acknowledge: it is easy to say that optimism and mindset play a defining role in success, and even easier to say if we come from a background of opportunity. I have been lucky enough to be able to consider the impact of factors like mindset on my everyday life without getting too much push-back from my circumstances. Starting my own company at the age of 20 alongside university would have been considerably more difficult for me had I been working long night shifts and stressing about making ends meet every day. I had the privilege of being able to try out various easy side jobs, with the regular anxieties of a university student, but also with the near-certainty that my livelihood wouldn't be threatened if things didn't work out. Thanks to the position I was in, I was confident that if a job did not work out, I would find something else. That is not the case for everyone and, of course, the more you have to fight against external circumstances, the harder it is to remain optimistic. Failures assume more meaning because they are more directly threatening. The opportunities you are afforded throughout your life – whether because of the country you live in, your family, your education or other parameters – have a great impact on how you view success and failure today. That definitely does not mean success is unattainable, it just means it might take more effort. Recognize that the successes you see around you are almost never presented whole – next time you compare yourself to a 12-year-old millionaire on TikTok, make sure to keep that in mind. Any time you think you are not doing or achieving enough, stop and consider: enough for whom? Under what circumstances? Give yourself some credit for even asking these questions, reading this book and searching for ways to create a life you are happy with. You're doing great – and no, you do not have to have it all figured out by your mid-20s; surprising as it is for Gen Z, life doesn't actually end after we turn 30 (or so I've been told).

Societal pressures and external validation

In many cases, even if you manage to redefine what success means to you, you still have to deal with external pressures. They can often be a strong force – every generation has its own points of focus when it comes to what is considered successful, so people around you can sometimes cause doubts, pressure and stress even if they want to be supportive. If you decide to take a leap and pursue an unconventional career, you might have to face the opinions of others who believe that it's not a viable career path and that you should get a 'real' job. This is to be expected – pursuing an alternative career in entrepreneurship, side gigs or something similar is not the norm. But the norm is never going to be the best option for everyone. Your alternative pathway can cause friction simply because it won't be relatable for many people around you. You will have to come to terms with hearing a flurry of frustrating misconceptions about these career paths. You may find yourself prompted to defend your choices more, to explain yourself to others, at least until you reach a point that they can more easily fit into their definition of success. But just because it is the road less travelled, it doesn't mean it is the wrong road to take.

Many people get sucked into traditional careers that don't suit them because they view their professional life as a linear path on which they need to keep up with their peers. But unconventional careers often require experimentation and reinvention which leads to a no-nlinear pathway. I see friends consumed by anxieties of wasting time in jobs they are uncertain about, eager to have it all figured out. In my eyes, these periods of experimentation and uncertainty, these jumps from one thing to the other, are helpful in a way we rarely recognize. They help you figure out a lot of things that are crucial for you to know: what you enjoy doing, what you thought seemed right for you but does not feel right after all, what new direction you might want to take. Working at a startup for a while might show you that you enjoy the fast-paced environment or you might find that it does not allow you to work how you work best. Either way, you haven't wasted your time. If you feel like you have spent too long stuck in jobs you did not like, then I suggest reframing that into a real learning experience and consciously seraching for the insights it gave you into your work preferences. That already puts you one step ahead because it gives you invaluable information that you can use to create your ideal career. I like to think of it like this: you are like a mosaic artist, collecting little pieces of tile and glass throughout your life that may seem 'useless' or unappealing by themselves. This is you collecting different career experiences while you are young – each job or project you try out, no matter how it ends up or how much you enjoy it, is a piece of that mosaic. Considered by themselves, you might not see any value in those pieces, but together they form the beautiful final mosaic, which is your ideal career. Every job adds colour, texture and value to the big picture – it reveals insights about what you do and do not want in your career path, contributing significantly to the final image.

Now, in order to deal with the external expectations and pressures that often make their way into our mind subconsciously, my first tip is to find a community that is on a similar journey. If you want to start your own company, find entrepreneurs online that have similar journeys to you (e.g. have started from a corporate job and moved on to entrepreneurship, if that is your case), and reach out to them to see if they are open to a call. A lot of people still remain open to giving some of their time to speaking to others that want advice to embark on a similar journey, even if they are very busy. If you are thinking of starting a side gig alongside your main job, then you can find people that have done that instead, and have managed to scale their side gig successfully, and reach out. I have noticed a trend among entrepreneurs, especially in the tech community, who make a point of responding to all the emails they get or who have a time every week on their calendar dedicated to speaking with different people. For example, entrepreneur and author Derek Sivers responds to every email he gets, and encourages his readers to get in touch. After reading a couple of his books, I emailed him to express my appreciation for some of the insights he shared in his books and ask a follow-up question, to which he promptly responded with a useful answer. Of course, many people will not reply at all, but it is worth trying – if there is someone you especially admire for some reason, send them a message and see what happens, you have nothing to lose. Even if not to jump on a call, many people are open to at least responding to questions they receive via message.

Also, do not underestimate the impact of finding a community that you can join. It can provide invaluable support and guidance during your career journey. Meeting like-minded people can be life-changing, and if you are surrounded only by people on completely different paths to yours, the journey will likely be more difficult. There are communities you can join centred around connecting like-minded people through online and in-person events. For example, Female Founder World is a global community of female entrepreneurs. Word Tonic is another online community specifically for Gen Z copywriters. There is something for everyone, and their goal is to facilitate connection and support, which is crucial when taking the path less travelled. Community is a support system. Entrepreneurship, freelancing, side gigs – they can easily become lonely pursuits but they do not have to be. By now, there are enough communities and channels out there that you can follow to access whole networks doing what you do.

Through social media, we have become addicted to external validation. How many times have you caught yourself thinking about your latest achievement and how you would announce it online or add it to your LinkedIn? It is only natural, considering how much of that we see every day. But we get too caught up in the announcements, the visibility and the external reactions. All it does is put our focus on the wrong metrics for success (in this case, likes, comments, congratulations), but this is not where success lies. It takes a conscious effort to free yourself from caring about how people on social media perceive your work and your achievements. Sharing the things you do is important because it can support your career, but if it stresses you out a lot, it might mean that you are defining yourself by your achievements and turning them into an identity. So then every time someone criticizes or disagrees with your path, it feels like a personal attack rather than a mere difference in opinions. Dissociate success from external validation and remember that real success is when you feel like you have succeeded, not when others do. It truly has nothing to do with the validation you get from others. When you reflect on what success looks like to you, I am certain you will find that it does not revolve around how other people perceive it. Success is personal because you live in it – it is about internal validation, not external. Making that dissociation has to be an intentional effort, so catch yourself next time you have these thoughts, and every time after that. Celebrating your wins with others is important, motivating and rewarding. But it should not be one of your driving factors. Keep reminding yourself how little social media announcements and validation really matter in the bigger picture of living a successful life, because chances are your social media feed will only keep pointing you in the other direction.

When I picture what success looks like to me, it is not so much about specific achievements as it is about living an everyday life that I truly enjoy. That in itself is the highest achievement to me, but it is not one I can announce on social media or add to my LinkedIn. The achievements I care about the most in the greater picture of my life, like having the time to pursue my passions and inspiration, are not the kind you get to announce on social media. 'Happy to announce that today I had time to read a book' probably won't go LinkedIn viral. Although, they might result in more tangible achievements as a consequence; for example, being able to dedicate a lot of my time to writing, also means I am now writing a book, which is a more tangible achievement. The everyday achievements that you cannot announce or quantify are still a very valid measure of success. Instead of only allowing yourself to feel successful when your success is directly measurable, you have to also account for all the everyday moments that contribute to you living your dream life. Often enough, appreciating the smaller everyday achievements is the only way to achieve significant levels of success in the future – without that, we tend to lose drive and motivation to go on and achieve our bigger goals. To reach the finish line, you have to be able to find satisfaction and validation before the final destination is reached. At the same time, having tangible goals that you are aiming to reach is also extremely important, because when you set specific goals, you are far more likely to reach them (42 per cent more likely to be exact, when you actually write them down!).[8] But you do not want your internal measure of success to entirely depend on whether you reach those goals or not, or whether you can announce them on LinkedIn. In order to stay sane, productive and happy, you need to recognize and celebrate the process just as much. The goals you set need to also include things you can do every day that make you feel happy and fulfilled, because, after all, your life is an accumulation of the days you live, not of the milestones you achieve. If you do not find the time to enjoy the present moment, how can you look back at your life and know it was well lived? Goals and success are a combination of the moments that make up every day, and the specific achievements you reach. We need to reframe the way we think about success as a whole to recognize both, and not put the emphasis only on the achievements themselves.

Arianna Huffington said it best: 'We need to accept that we won't always make the right decisions, that we'll screw up royally sometimes — understanding that failure is not the opposite of success, it's part of success.'[9] Redefining our relationship with success and failure is an essential prerequisite to creating our ideal career, and therefore our ideal life. If you take one thing from this chapter, make it this: only you can define what success means for you, and it is an exercise that you absolutely should engage in if you are trying to build a life on your terms. Try not to be influenced by all the definitions of success you see around you, but rather focus internally and go based on your personal values and priorities. Whether you are more driven by purpose, passion, freedom, security or something else is something you have to clarify in your mind. It will guide you in figuring out what type of career would work best for you, and it has a tangible impact on the decisions you will make. If security is one of your highest values, you can definitely still pursue a 'riskier', entrepreneurial path, it might just mean that you will choose a business model or industry that has lower risk than someone who is happy going all out and risking everything for a higher reward. It's completely up to you. There are infinite different paths you can follow. The choice might seem overwhelming, after all. Where do you even start? In my opinion, this is where. You first have to face the big picture to understand what road to take.

Notes

1   Habit Better (2020) We've got 99 Reasons to Journal... here are your top 7. https://habitbetter.com/top-ranked-benefits-of-journaling/ (archived at https://perma.cc/M9WR-6L3Y)

2   Anderer, J (2022) Remote work doesn't lower productivity, can even boost resilience, study says, Study Finds. https://studyfinds.org/remote-work-productivity/ (archived at https://perma.cc/22JK-8VGA)

3   Laker, B (2023) Remote work is less productive: Study, Psychology Today. www.psychologytoday.com/us/blog/mindful-leadership/202308/remote-work-is-less-productive-study (archived at https://perma.cc/3LUR-3KVW)

4   Dweck, C (2006) *Mindset: The new psychology of success*, Random House, New York

5   Forbes (2023) ForbesQuotes, www.forbes.com/quotes/6315/ (archived at perma.cc/5PLK-5STD)

6   Dweck, C (2006) *Mindset: The new psychology of success*, Random House, New York

7   Tiayon, S B (2021) How optimism helps you achieve goals with less stress, Greater Good Magazine. https://greatergood.berkeley.edu/article/item/how_optimism_helps_you_achieve_goals_with_less_stress (archived at https://perma.cc/BS8P-FWGH)

8   Economy, P (2018) This is the way you need to write down your goals for faster success, Inc. www.inc.com/peter-economy/this-is-way-you-need-to-write-down-your-goals-for-faster-success.html (archived at https://perma.cc/ZDD3-42SB)

9   Huffington, A @ariannahuff (2019), Twitter/X, twitter.com/ariannahuff/status/1130172552352063489?s=21 (archived at https://perma.cc/UG7E-GAVW)

CHAPTER THREE

Big gigs and side gigs

The rise of side gigs and independent work

It's time to get down to the practical level of what it could mean to restructure your career, and how. Assuming you cannot just quit your current job or drop out of university to begin your dream project, there are more realistic ways to get started that are broadly accessible. Many entrepreneurs and successful self-employed people got where they are after balancing and testing multiple things, and it is increasingly common today to begin this journey with a side gig (or side hustle). A side gig is basically a job that you do outside of your regular job, and it can be anything from freelancing, to having your own startup, to a digital product or service that gives you an additional source of passive income, to many other possibilities that we will explore in this chapter. We will discuss popular types of independent work, their benefits and unique characteristics, as well as specific examples of successful case studies to draw inspiration and learn from. You will learn about service-based gigs, agencies, digital products and productized agencies, as well as SaaS startups, e-commerce and content-based gigs, which are allowing creators to make a living doing what they love. Through interviews with young independent professionals succeeding in their own path, you will also read about alternative ways people are finding to work for themselves and structure work on their terms. Some of these examples present paths that many people may not even know are possible, so hopefully their stories will educate or inspire you.

The numbers behind the rise of side gigs might surprise you: in the UK, 70 per cent of Gen Zers have a side gig.[1] In the US, 50 per cent of Millennials do as well. One misconception is that those numbers are as high as they are because people need additional sources of income – while that is true for a lot of people, especially younger ones, research shows that 50 per cent of people with a side gig do it because they want to, not because of a financial need.[2] Today, side gigs have become a way for millions of people to pursue passion projects, and to work towards their dream career alongside the safety net of a 'regular' job. In my case, my company was a side gig for a couple of years before it became my main job. I first ran it alongside university, and then alongside my postgraduate studies and my full-time remote job. Having multiple things going on at once made it feel like a side gig, even though most of my creative energy, passion and interest were still going into it. The safety net of my main job allowed me to build my company from the ground up without the pressure and anxiety of having it be my only source of income, which was definitely helpful as I was figuring out how to build a team, scale a company and plan a big-picture strategy.

While I did feel some internal pressure to make it my main job as soon as I could, I also think it was helpful to build a company without rushing to make profit the number one priority from day one – it allowed me to build well thought-out systems, and make sure we were set up to produce high-quality work first and foremost. If you are very ambitious, starting with a side gig might seem unappealing, like you are not moving fast enough, but there are many such benefits that we will explore later on that make it a great way to begin. I also believe there is an added element of efficiency introduced to one's work when it is done as a side gig alongside other jobs or studies, specifically because of the limited time that you can allocate to it. Side gigs force you to work smarter, not harder, and that is one of the most beneficial skills you can learn in the long term to build a successful career.

'Independent work', as a whole, refers to being self-employed, most commonly through something like freelancing. Independent work does not have to be a side gig – it often starts as that, alongside a main job, but then becomes the main job itself once you reach a level of work that is sustainable. Independent work is quickly rising in popularity: in the US, 36 per cent of employed workers say they work independently, either full time or as a side gig.[3] In 2016, it was just 27 per cent. All the research points towards the conclusion that independent work will continue to rise, and will become a much bigger part of the job market than many might expect. A common misconception is that working for yourself is less secure. Interestingly, since the Covid-19 pandemic, many people now see traditional jobs as less secure. Independent workers are reporting feeling a lot more secure when they have their own business of some kind, which offers much-needed peace of mind among corporate layoffs and job market fluctuations.[4]

In most types of independent work, it is indeed more difficult to suddenly lose your livelihood compared to traditional jobs. While there is more pressure on you to sustain the work, you can be reassured that you won't be suddenly laid off or made redundant like you might as a traditional employee. Freelancers tend to also have more than one client, so their range of work is diversified, splitting their income between many different sources. In independent work, you have much more control over your circumstances. Instead of having to prove to a superior that you deserve to keep your job or rise to a promotion, you instead focus on scaling your own work and the results can be a lot more immediate, rewarding and impactful. Financially, the numbers are also increasing every year; a study conducted in 2022 found that 4.4 million American independent workers are earning over $100,000 per year. Successful self-employment is not rare; it may actually be a lot more common than you think.

The benefits of independent work

This increase in independent work and side gigs represents a wider shift in priorities among workers and is impacting society as a whole. It is a good time to be thinking about how you can create a career structure that really works for you, because alternative types of work are becoming more widespread and normalized. As we saw in the last chapter, there is a rise in people prioritizing ownership, which independent work ties into. Autonomy, flexibility, ownership and control have assumed much greater importance in people's employment choices than they used to and more people are recognizing that independent work is the best pathway to gaining that ownership If you are currently trying to figure out whether your ideal career lies in a traditional job or in independent work, this should help you clear up some common doubts you might be having.

First, independent workers see a much higher level of job satisfaction. Not only that, but they report feeling healthier and having improved wellbeing as a result of working for themselves. This is a significant pattern: 87 per cent of independent workers report feeling happier, and 80 per cent report better health as a result of doing this type of work compared to traditional employment.[5] Does that sound too good to be true? Truth is, having more control over your work-life balance can make a huge difference in your everyday life and wellbeing. In most types of independent work, you can control your daily schedule more than in traditional jobs. One reason why so many independent workers could never imagine going back to a regular job is because once you start incorporating more good habits into your day, such as being able to take breaks and go on morning walks, or using time saved from not commuting on hobbies and quality time, it becomes indispensable. Being independent can also grant you greater creative freedom, which is essential for most creatives to feel satisfied with their job. It is harder to fully explore and express your creativity in a traditional job, where your responsibilities, scope and the initiatives you work on are usually more limited. For those who really value creative freedom and independence, it is likely that working for yourself would result in a more fulfilling work life. Considering independent work as a career structure is a solid step towards creating your ideal career – it is first about understanding the nature and benefits of independent work itself, and then about figuring out what type of such job would be best for you.

Along with having control of your time, another benefit is efficiency. I am one of those people who think about efficiency a lot – I get frustrated easily when I have to work in inefficient systems, and I realize how much it takes away from my potential to do my best work and feel good doing it. The truth is that a lot of traditional jobs are often full of inefficiencies: for example, measuring the success of your work and performance in input versus output, so that the hours you put in matter more than the quality of work you do. Measuring performance in input definitely makes sense for some industries, but for many it doesn't. Traditional 9–5 jobs are usually based on input: employees are expected to work a certain number of hours, regardless of the actual outcomes of their work. Their presence in the office during those hours is taken as a sign of commitment and evaluated as an important metric; it is common for office-based 9–5 workers to have nothing to do, but to have to spend those hours there anyway.

For these types of jobs, assessing performance based on time spent working seems inefficient. Instead, companies that focus on output-based assessments value what you achieved more than how long you spent achieving it. That also motivates employees more, because they focus on doing impactful work and taking initiatives rather than just killing time because their output doesn't make a difference to their career. For independent workers, such as freelancers in marketing, software development or design, the output is what matters – they work on delivering a project and it does not matter to the client how long they spent on it. It therefore feels like their time is spent a lot more efficiently, without the pressure of sitting at an office and waiting for something to come up. Spending eight hours in an office does not mean that the work produced is of higher quality than it would have been if it was done in a flexible environment in half the time. Also, spending eight hours in an office does not in any way mean a person is being productive. How many people can actually do real, focused work for eight hours straight in a 9–5? Instead of considering how people work and focus best, these traditional jobs focus on the hours and forget about actual productivity. This is one problem that independent work can solve. The job satisfaction rates among independent workers are so high partly because people feel like when they work, they work, and when they have no work to do or they do not feel productive, they can instead use their time however they like. It makes more sense to be able to structure your workflow around specific goals and deliverables, and to measure success based on the quality of your work rather than on how well you managed to stick to a strict schedule.

The next benefit is the financial one. Independent work is far more scalable than traditional jobs. In a traditional job, the pace in which you can scale the amount of money you earn is a lot slower and more fixed. There isn't much room for flexibility, and often people are stuck in the frustrating reality of having to go through the set steps of a corporate ladder, even when they are skilled enough to do much more. The consulting and investment banking industries are a good example of this: consultants often start as analysts or associates straight out of university, and remain in this role for one–two years on average, spending their time carrying out laborious busywork that doesn't make use of their skillset. I interviewed a 24-year-old consultant at a leading firm who told me that they spend hours on tasks that could be automated, such as transcribing calls. This mechanical and unsatisfying work left them feeling drained on a daily basis:

> The intensity of that work leaves no space for my mind to have any thoughts, so I feel like at the end of the day, I am exhausted not just because of the long hours, but because of the lack of engagement. In large firms, promotions and responsibility come with tenure rather than with skill. You have a very defined path before you can advance to the next stage, and even then, the increase in responsibility and interest in your work is going to be only incremental. Your promotion doesn't feel like a promotion, because the work remains so

similar. At the end of the day, the financial reward doesn't even feel worth it – if you had invested the same amount of time and years in building a business instead, it is possible you would have earned that amount of money faster.

They also report it being an environment of very high stress, due to the focus on maximizing profit for others as efficiently as possible: 'Instead of working so profusely for others for pennies on the dollar, I would like to create my own structure, and be more directly connected to the fruits of my labour.' We are seeing a shift in young workers prioritizing the scalability and potential of their work more than before, in a way traditional corporate jobs cannot allow. Switching to independent work means that you can work smarter to earn more money, and most importantly, that you feel that your daily work has a direct impact on getting you to where you want to go. Instead of feeling stuck on a fixed ladder, you can see that your work will make a tangible difference much faster.

Another benefit is the scope of experiences that you can gather as an independent worker. If you are a graphic designer, for example, and you work at a company, it is likely you will spend years working within a limited scope: same company, same branding, same types of projects. As a freelance designer, on the other hand, in one year's worth of work you can have produced a portfolio of dozens of vastly different projects. This both allows you to learn and grow a lot faster as a professional and also showcases the breadth of your skills in a tangible way, capturing your level of experience. The freelance designer may soon decide to turn their business into a design studio, beginning to employ other people and building a team of designers to work on larger projects and achieve more ambitious goals. In that case, the portfolio that showcases various experiences is helpful: it builds credibility that is essential in creative industries. The broad range of experiences you gather is also extremely helpful in figuring out what you love spending time on, and what you do not enjoy as much. Independent work can allow you to explore a lot more easily. With each exploration, you come closer to understanding what your ideal type of career would be. This exposure to varying experiences is valuable, especially when you are young and your focus is on better understanding your work preferences. Working on multiple projects is a learning experience that may offer you more than a traditional job can. It also allows you to develop your skills a lot faster, especially as you assume more and more responsibility and scale the level of your services whenever you want. Another result of this is market adaptability: as a freelancer, you get to work across many different industries (unless you intentionally decide to specialize). You get to gain experience within a broad range of sectors, which means that if an industry slows down because of market fluctuations at some point, that doesn't influence you because you can more easily pivot to another.

I also find that working for myself has given me access to a significantly larger network than I ever had before. Meeting new people working on exciting new initiatives became very common, and, at least in my industry, I never had that level of exposure to new people in any of my traditional jobs. So, the networking aspect of independent work can often be an unexpected and rewarding part of it.

The networking sources seem to only be increasing as my business grows: working with different clients around the world, taking calls with prospective clients and partners, speaking to people interested in joining our team, speaking at events around the world and meeting dozens of people at every one of them, and meeting fellow Gen Z founders through online communities. When you are an independent worker, you often become more visible, and thus attract more like-minded people. You can still meet tons of people while working a traditional job, but in my experience it has been slower and more constrained. Collaborating with new people is exciting exactly because it is easy: so many times I have met young entrepreneurs working on interesting businesses, and have then decided to join our forces and create some initiatives together. When you are in control, you can make such decisions easily, and expand the way you collaborate with others. The more your business grows, the more people you get to meet – and networking is one of the most impactful things you can do for your career, simply because you *never know* what doors it can open in the future. In other words, being more visible by working for yourself puts you in a position where you are more likely to attract serendipity. By exposing yourself to a larger network of people and fellow independent workers, you can attract opportunities, collaborations and life-changing connections.

The benefits of side gigs

All of these benefits apply to independent work in general. If you are in a position where you can't just start working for yourself and switch to independent work, then side gigs are the best way forward. If you have a main job that leaves you a little time you can use towards a side gig, it can be a great way to start transitioning towards an independent career, even if you only do it for a couple of hours every week. The first benefit of side gigs, specifically, is that they can start simple but then turn into your main stream of income. You can start alongside the safety of a regular job without having to take a big entrepreneurial leap, and work consistently and smartly to build your side gig into a scalable and viable job. With side gigs, you do not have to have everything figured out from the start. You can use the security of it being just a side gig to test and experiment with different ideas and business models without the pressure of it having to work out. Then, with consistent effort and with all the insight you gather from testing different things, you can arrive at a point where your side job has reached or surpassed your main stream of income, which is when many independent workers decide to quit their main job and focus on their own work full time. Of course, you can argue that full-time independent work from the start allows you to commit all of your time to growing your own business, which can make it succeed much faster. That is definitely true. There is no single best way to launch an independent career, so the most useful thing is to understand the benefits of each type of work, and evaluate what is most feasible and appealing to you.

Starting with a side gig is also beneficial as it is the best way for you to transform your passion into a career, without the pressure of it having to be your full-time job. This is more difficult if you go straight into independent work because your first priority is to make it profitable and successful quickly, to ensure you have a consistent stream of income. Thanks to social media, the prospect of transforming your side gig passion into a fully fledged career is easier than ever. Sharing your passions and personal projects online, if you are lucky, can make you go viral or allow you to reach people who are willing to pay for what you do. There are infinite ways this can happen: if you have a creative hobby like photography or film, sharing your work online can turn into a real business once you get traction. If your passion is something like building apps or games for fun, sharing those on social media can reach people who are willing to pay to use them, and then you can monetize them and turn them into a business. When your livelihood does not depend on it, you get to pursue your passions without stress, following what truly inspires you and thus producing your best-quality work. That is a huge benefit of side gigs. Instead of feeling the pressure of having to immediately quit your job and start something of your own, you can use the fact that you have a regular source of income to experiment with your passions and the projects that fully, deeply interest and fulfil you alongside that. Those types of projects tend to turn into the most fulfilling types of careers, because they are driven by a real interest and intrinsic drive.

The challenges of independent work

While offering flexibility and autonomy, as well as the freedom to build your dream life, independent work also comes with some challenges that are worth acknowledging. A lack of job security and predictable income is something a lot of independent workers struggle with. While it spreads your income between different sources or projects, this type of work can still be unstable if it is not supported by the right systems. That is why, for freelancers, talent marketplaces like Upwork and Fiverr provide a way to create more consistency around your work: they can allow you to create a system for applying and getting new jobs regularly, lowering your chances of being left without work. Talent marketplaces can also incentivize clients and freelancers to keep working together long term, by providing features that facilitate this and allow workers to build relationships with their clients.[6] They help freelancers market their services, and provide a lot of the features needed to highlight their work and experience. Using such platforms rather than going out there completely on your own can help you mitigate this challenge and increase the chances of having a consistent workload.

Another challenge is the additional risk that can come with independent work and its lack of structure compared to traditional jobs. For example, unclear contracts, clients that disappear without paying and intellectual property conflicts can arise. To mitigate that, freelancers should ensure they are on top of their business's legal side, putting contracts in place that will protect them and their work. Talent marketplaces can also protect workers from occurrences like these, as they often have ways to prevent non-payment and disappearing clients, and provide standard contracts. It is important to recognize all these risks and make sure that you know exactly how you are protecting yourself from being exposed through potential situations like these.

Service-based gigs

Perhaps the easiest type of independent work to start with is a service-based one. That includes freelancing, as well as business models such as agencies, which are basically more scalable versions of freelancing. Providing a service as a contractor is one of the easiest ways to begin working for yourself. You just need to identify what skill you have that is in enough demand, or what skill you could learn that is in demand (see the examples mentioned in Chapter 1). A few years ago, providing a service as a freelancer had a higher barrier for entry, because it was harder to find clients to work with, prove your credibility and ensure a consistent stream of income from this type of work. Today, however, you can literally get your first client from one day to the next. Platforms like Upwork, Fiverr and Contra connect freelancers with people hiring for all kinds of jobs, and the rate of jobs uploaded on those platforms is quick enough that you can always find someone that is looking for the skills you have.

New jobs are constantly being uploaded, and even though there is a lot of competition on these platforms, you can stand out without much difficulty because there is also a lot of spam. As someone who hires often enough through Upwork for various tasks, if I receive 30 proposals, 10 or more of them are usually spam, where they clearly have not read my actual requirements. So, when I see a proposal from someone who seems legit and has experience, I hire them. If you focus on tailoring your proposal to what the jobs are asking for instead of copy-pasting the same generic text, you have high chances of getting hired and landing your first client. With freelance gigs, people will also often take a chance on you even when you do not have much visible experience. When I was 19 and working part-time social media marketing jobs, I decided to try and see if I could get a freelance client. On my second day of applying to relevant jobs, I got hired by someone who I ended up working with for almost two years, even after I launched my marketing agency. She hired me even though I had no ratings on the platform yet, based on nothing but what I wrote in my proposal. So, even for beginners, these platforms are friendly and accessible enough to make it almost a guarantee that if you write enough thoughtful proposals, someone will take a chance on you. If you are not sure where to start, it does not matter that much which freelance platform you choose, but I find they do have some key differences from the freelancer's side.

On Upwork, you create a profile with your skills and relevant experience, and then browse through jobs and apply using 'Connects'. Connects are like points you have to pay for in order to apply to jobs. But don't let that put you off; the pricing is good value based on how many applications it corresponds to. On Fiverr, you can create a profile with the specific services you offer, and people can directly come and buy your services. It is quite a different structure, where you can offer various packages and tiers of services with different pricing. Then, if someone wants to hire a social media strategist and you have a profile offering social media strategy, especially if you have positive client reviews on your profile and your offering looks legitimate, they can just buy it as they would a product. All you have to do is deliver the work.

The good thing about Fiverr's structure is that if you invest time on the platform and you start getting a lot of jobs from there, you become a higher-ranked seller and then it is easier to secure new jobs and upscale the services you offer. Finally, there's Contra, a relatively new platform that is more focused on Gen Z – its aesthetic is a lot more appealing to young contractors, and it has an online community for them to connect with each other, learn and access opportunities. Because of its less generic nature (it looks very much like a platform built for a younger and tech-savvy audience), the jobs posted on Contra also tend to be more curated. That is, on platforms like Upwork you will also find thousands of jobs that pay very little or that just want someone to complete dull tasks, while the companies that post on Contra are more likely to be offering opportunities that will be specific to your skillset – allowing you to more effectively develop your skills and build your portfolio. They also have a feature that allows freelancers to build a portfolio website on the platform, making it easy to share and curate their best work. What I love about freelance work is that it has become incredibly accessible for so many different types of services. Freelance can be a lot more than the typical creative jobs like graphic design or marketing, you can offer services such as software development, translation, project management, virtual assistance, copyediting, SEO, data analysis, tutoring on any kind of subject and even jobs like financial consulting. Anything you are good at, you can probably offer as some type of service.

Pros of service-based gigs:

- Work-life balance: As a freelancer, you can set your own schedule and do your work on your own terms.
- Opportunity for higher income: Scaling the level of your income to match your experience as a freelancer is easier than in traditional jobs, where you have to go through set paths to get promoted and grow.
- Development of multiple skills: This type of work is similar to running a business, where you develop a skillset beyond what you would in a traditional job. Time management skills, financial skills and sales skills are all essential for freelancers.

Cons of service-based gigs:

- No paid time off: Freelancers don't typically get paid time off, as they get paid for the hours of work they do or the projects they complete. So, any time off affects their income.
- Lack of consistency and security: As mentioned earlier, in this type of independent work it can sometimes be challenging to ensure a consistent workflow and regular income.

From freelancer to founder

However, while freelancing is a great way to start working independently and figuring out where there is an overlap of market demand and your skills and passions, it is not the best long-term solution if you have more ambitious goals. With freelancing, you are exchanging your time for money. No matter how high your rates can get after years of experience, you still have to sell the limited amount of time you have in a day. That means that it is not a very scalable business model – it is very difficult to build wealth with freelancing. If one of your goals is true financial freedom, there is only so far that a freelance job can scale. Instead, the next step for many freelancers is to turn their work into a company, usually an agency of some sort. Whereas when you are a freelancer the asset is you, when you invest the same amount of time instead into growing a business of your own, then the business becomes the asset. That means that you can scale it, and if it goes well you can eventually even sell it. Then, you are no longer exchanging your time for money. You build systems that can work without you, and your involvement can be focused on bigger-picture strategy and scaling the business, rather than on client-facing work and day-to-day tasks. Then the hours you spend working are more dependent on you: you are not just doing reactive tasks, such as delivering work to clients, but proactive tasks, activities which will grow the business but that are usually not time-sensitive. Your time becomes more flexible and free, to use as you like.

While owning a business of any kind still requires a lot of work, service-based agencies are one of the simplest business models you can have. Their structure is very straightforward, and in most cases you do not need funding in order to begin. When you get a client, you usually have the margin you need, as running costs are not as high as in many other types of companies, for example those selling physical products. Agencies can easily function remotely, so you do not need an office, and there are so many resources out there to find out how to structure your operating processes for maximum efficiency. There are countless agencies offering everything related to marketing, web development, design and a lot more, but if you find a way to differentiate your offering or stand out among the competition, you have a good chance of succeeding. Just do not make the mistake of trying to scale too fast – you need to master the art of maintaining a high quality of work first, in a way that won't be compromised when you grow. Finally, it is a huge advantage if you understand branding and marketing inside and out. If you manage to nail your company's branding and create a recognizable and loveable brand around it, you can then expand on to other types of offerings too. By building a name that people get to know and trust, your company can evolve alongside you over time, making it easier for it to develop in new directions that interest you instead of staying stagnant.

Of course, going from offering a specific service to running a company requires new skills; but no one is born with them, so it is nothing you can't learn. You will need to understand how to build and manage a team, become a better leader, navigate company finances and operations. You can always work with people who will be better at these things than you, but as a founder it is essential to have a certain level of understanding to stay on top of your business. So, if you go down the freelance path, consider how eventually turning it into a business can give you more ownership, autonomy and freedom over your work.

Pros of agencies:

- Scalability: Compared to traditional freelancing, agencies can grow a lot more, and a lot faster. As they are not limited by one person's time like traditional freelancing, they can grow alongside the demand.
- Greater freedom and flexibility: An agency business model allows you to build a team instead of doing everything yourself, providing countless ways to automate the business's processes and remove yourself from the day-to-day tasks if you wish to.

Cons of agencies:

- Complex operations: Successfully running an agency model requires excellent operations and maximum efficiency, which can be difficult to perfect and is where many such companies fail.

Digital products

Digital products are one type of independent work that is currently becoming increasingly popular. Its appeal is in the fact that it can become a passive income stream, which, as long as you can market it successfully, can grow to become very profitable. You only need to create a digital product once, and you can sell it forever. Creating digital products also does not have high running costs. A lot of digital products can be created for free, making the barrier for entry low as well. In 2020, an estimated two billion people bought digital products.[7] The versatility of this category appears to only be growing, with social media platforms such as TikTok helping a lot of digital-product-based businesses around the world skyrocket. If they meet a real need or understand how to fully appeal to a specific segment of people, digital products can have great potential as a business model. They are usually priced either as a subscription or as a one-off payment.

There are countless different pathways to take in the creation of digital products. One of the most popular is that of educational digital products, which includes ebooks, online courses, webinars and interactive tools. Online courses and webinars are quickly growing in popularity – 70 per cent of students believe that online methods of learning are more effective than conventional ones.[8] This increase in popularity has led the online education market to grow significantly in recent years, pushing educational digital products forward. Another leading category is business and productivity-related digital products: this includes things like Excel spreadsheets for sale, digital templates and tools to facilitate marketing, business or legal activities. There are many niche subcategories of digital products as well, which have turned into entire successful businesses serving a very specific target market.

One of the most common types is online courses. I will mention these alongside ebooks because they both work in the same way: they are usually educational, and they offer buyers a way to purchase a single product once, which will teach them all they need to know on a certain topic. Whether it is done through a downloadable ebook or as a video-based course, these educational resources are tried and tested, and there are endless topics they can cover. Ebooks are simpler – if you sell a service or provide knowledge of some kind, you can create a 30–50 page ebook that combines all the knowledge that people would find most useful on a topic, and sell it on a platform like Gumroad, Etsy or on your own website or landing page. Ebooks are usually only viable if you have already built some credibility around a certain topic. In order to sell, you need to have positioned yourself as an expert on the topic that people know they can trust.

So, even though they are simple enough to create, ebooks first require the effort of building a trustworthy personal brand. The difference in online courses, besides the format, is that they can more easily become 'premium' products. For online courses with a proven record of happy buyers, and a community around them to confirm its quality and value, prices can range from $2,000–$9,000 per customer. One example is Write of Passage, a writing course by David Perell that teaches students how to write online. It sells from $3,995–$6,995 for lifetime access. Write of Passage has seen great success, due to its hundreds of happy students and the community that has been created around it on social media. It has therefore managed to establish credibility, which is also supported by David Perell's own social media presence, as he is prolific in the online writing space. Building an audience that knows you and trusts you as an expert on a topic is a huge advantage, and it opens the door to selling educational digital products. Ebooks are still priced low enough to be impulsive purchases, so with social media ads, if an ebook meets a real need it can still manage to sell without any pre-established credibility. With online courses, that would hardly work, so creators rarely start from that alone without having built a personal brand in some way first. But it is very rewarding and a great business model to consider after you have built a brand or a personal brand that people know they can trust.

Another interesting case study is that of Steph Smith, who left her consulting job and two-hour commute to pursue a more alternative path. She decided to learn to code using a $20 online course, and has built multiple products ever since that have ranked #1 on Product Hunt (a website featuring interesting products and tools that is very popular among the tech community). Smith's book, *Doing Content Right*, centres around online content creation. Smith's book launch was far from traditional: sitting somewhere between a book and a digital product, *Doing Content Right* had a successful launch as a 'resource that covers everything you need to know about publishing online'. Instead of selling as a standalone book, it sells as a digital product bundle for $150 that includes the 270-page ebook, recorded lessons, printable exercises, a community of creators, a quiz and a bonus audio section. It combines the best parts of building an online course, an ebook and a digital product, and is sold as a bundle to an audience that would benefit from all the parts included and be willing to invest in something like this. Having built other digital products as well since learning to code, Smith learned how to create digital content and products that sell, and mastered the art of building large, engaged audiences. With a strong personal brand and this skillset, it has opened many doors for Smith and allowed her to follow this unique path doing what she loves.

There has also been a lot of demand, in the past few years, for digital products revolving around templates. This includes templates for Notion, for Excel spreadsheets, even for legal documents. They are sold either individually or in bundles, and we have seen through prominent case studies that they can become very successful and profitable for creators. You can create a template once, and sell it indefinitely. The process is very simple and all you need to do is find the demand, solve a problem and create something people would find valuable and useful. For example, on Etsy there is a huge demand for downloadable digital planners and productivity tools, which are sold at price points usually between $5–$20. They allow users to instantly download them and start using them, most commonly on an iPad, to replace physical planners. The running costs are basically zero to sell this type of product, other than the social media ads they may run to boost their reach, so it has become a very competitive market.

Similarly, Notion templates meet this need but for a usually more entrepreneurial and tech-driven crowd. If you are not familiar with Notion, it is an app for all kinds of note taking and organization, very helpful for businesses, students or personal-use cases. It is very versatile and it allows you to create a workspace within which you organize notes with a lot of flexibility. While Notion provides its own free templates and you can also create your own, there is a large community of creators that make and sell templates that meet different needs, and differentiate themselves either through great design or functionality, usually both. Creating Notion templates is complicated and time-consuming, especially if you want to incorporate relational databases, task progress trackers and other useful tools, so many users would naturally prefer a ready-made solution that makes their life easier.

One of the most successful entrepreneurs selling Notion templates is Ruiyi Chin, who goes by the name Easlo. Only 21 years old at the time of writing, he built a follower base by providing free Notion templates, on Twitter/X, which appealed to those interested in productivity tools. Through his initial free offering, he established himself in the productivity/Notion niche, and amassed a very rapidly increasing following as a result. He then started creating paid templates, and, unsurprisingly, his followers were happy to pay to access them. Now, Easlo's Notion templates business makes over $500,000 in yearly revenue.[9] Solving a common problem and helping people become more productive through digital templates is therefore a very viable business for many creators out there. If you have a productivity system that seems to be working better than the people around you, consider turning it into a paid productivity resource, for example, through a template or planner. There are so many ways to turn it into a digital product, and it could become profitable quickly if you master the marketing aspect.

This category also includes social media templates. Designers and marketers can create a bundle of social media designs, for example, and target a specific industry with the aim of making social media management and content creation much easier for them. Haley Ingram's Coffee and Contracts is a business that provides social media templates and content ideas for real estate professionals, for a monthly subscription of $54.[10] With a yearly revenue of almost $2 million as of late 2023, it is a great example of how a subscription model meeting a niche audience's needs can turn into a very successful and profitable business. In an interview with Starter Story, Ingram explained that the business continues to grow at an average five per cent every month, promoted mainly through Instagram and affiliate referrals. Such a business model also has very low running costs, making it easily profitable thanks to its structure: according to Ingram, Coffee and Contracts has an average gross margin of 95 per cent.[11] Compare that to a lot of traditional business models that have high expenses due to physical products and tangible costs, resulting in very low margins, and digital products provide a way to harness the internet to access new entrepreneurial possibilities.

Pros of digital products:

- Profitability: Their low running costs and high profit margins make them a relatively easy type of business to grow.
- Scalability: With no concern around running out of stock, they are easily scalable and can be sold infinitely without the need for extra resources or inventory.
- Immediacy: Consumers love having the instant delivery that comes with purchasing digital products.
- Ease and accessibility: Most types of digital products do not require very advanced technical skills to put together, and the skills they do require are easy to develop with some practice.

Cons of digital products:

- Oversaturation: The ease of creating and selling digital products has made this market very competitive and oversaturated: you only need to take one look at the digital planner section on Etsy to see the overwhelming amount of near-identical products being sold, with no real way of standing out. It has become a crowded marketplace, and while it is easy to enter, it can be harder to grow.
- Competition: Competitors with high budgets to spend on marketing can easily outperform others, which can turn it into a numbers game. Like everything else in this chapter, it is a matter of learning to stand out by providing something different to a specific audience segment, and managing to market it in a way that does not just require a high budget to spend on ads, and can rely on valuable organic content to reach the right audience and scale sustainably.

Productized agencies

At the intersection of service-based work and digital products, sits a newer addition to the independent work world: productized agencies. Productized agencies basically take the typical agency model, offering services such as marketing or design, and turn it into a subscription-based digital product. The difference between that and a regular agency is that productized agencies sell their services as a ready-to-buy bundle, where for a fixed price every month, businesses can get an amount of agreed deliverables that is usually quite high, which is where the appeal is for many. Perhaps the most popular such agency is Designjoy – it gained popularity because it was one of the first to implement such a model, and it became a textbook example of how a one-person agency can become successful and make millions in revenue every year. The founder, Brett Williams, is very public on social media about how he runs DesignJoy, and about the company's financials. This has shown the public that there is indeed very high demand for such a service, and that brands are willing to pay a lot for it. In the case of DesignJoy, it appealed to brands by offering unlimited design requests (made one by one) for a monthly fee of $5,000.

Promising a short turnaround time and high quality, Brett managed to scale the company to $110,000 in monthly revenue (as of late 2023), and create a wave of new productized agencies testing out the same business model across different industries and price points. Brett also sells an online course teaching others how to do the same, called 'Productize Yourself: Make $25,000 per month by productizing what you're good at', with lessons teaching students how to replicate this business model and make it work successfully. The course itself makes $45,000 in monthly revenue at the time of writing, proving the value of selling a course offering insight to your audience when they already trust what you do and know they can learn from you. Designjoy remains (at least at the time of writing) a one-person team. That makes the running costs very low, but can also make it a busy job to ensure meeting every client's demands and delivering high-quality work on time. To remain a one-person team, such an agency caps the number of clients they can work with at any given time based on their capacity. Otherwise, they can expand into more of a traditional agency model, hiring a team and scaling alongside the demand.

There are various ways to run a productized agency, and it is still a new enough business model that I am sure we will have a lot of interesting case studies to see in the coming years. For some, the premise of offering *unlimited* requests to clients for a monthly fee may sound daunting, and for good reason – in such a business model, you have to define the ground rules very well, so clients do not feel misled. For DesignJoy, while requests can be unlimited, they have to be made one by one. In the usual agency model, the exact deliverables are pre-agreed between agency and client, so you rarely have an unexpected workload. It allows you to plan better. So, why create a productized agency? In my opinion the appeal for founders and service providers is that under the unlimited requests premise, you can charge higher fees a lot earlier in your career than you could as a typical agency. Clients understand the higher fee immediately and are more willing to accept it because having the option to request unlimited designs, unlimited marketing content or whatever your agency is offering, sounds too good to pass up. Productized agencies are still new enough that we do not have many different case studies to explore what success looks like for them in the long term, but it is early enough that it can be an interesting model to consider, especially in a niche that has not yet been oversaturated. You just have to find a way to differentiate yourself, and most importantly to ensure consistent quality alongside scale.

Pros of productized agencies:

- Simplified sales process: The productization part removes the usual sales cycle that exists in freelancing and traditional agencies.
- Easy upselling: As a product, it is easier to upsell existing clients by offering higher-tier subscriptions.
- High rates: Depending on the appeal of the productized deliverables, these agencies can charge higher rates more quickly.

Cons of productized agencies:

- Limited personalization: Traditional agencies can benefit a lot from tailoring packages to clients' specific needs, while productized agencies sell set deliverables without customizing them for each new client.
- Operational challenges: In models that offer unlimited deliverables, the operations are a lot more complex to set up to ensure everything remains manageable.
- Higher churn rates: The productization part and the set deliverables make it likely that more clients will churn if they do not constantly need the services they are paying for.

SaaS startups

Then, of course, we can't talk about common side gigs and independent work without mentioning one of the most typical startup business models: SaaS (software as a service). They are exactly what they sound like: this category includes any brand selling a software as a service. You likely use some type of SaaS every day: Stripe for making or accepting payments online, WeTransfer for transferring files and so on. If you know how to code, SaaS startups are a common avenue for those who are also entrepreneurial and want to build tools others can use. That is why coding is one of the most useful skills you can learn right now – if you spot a problem, you can *build* the solution, and that is how a lot of SaaS startups are born. SaaS startups are very versatile and offer a lot of different avenues for monetization, and depending on the nature of the product, you can run some paid ads to quickly check if there is general interest in your idea. Converting a viewer into a user can have quite a low barrier in such products, which makes it easier for founders to determine whether they have product–market fit and are working on a sustainable idea that could become successful. With the rise of AI-powered coding tools as well as no-code tools, experimenting with SaaS products is quickly becoming a lot more accessible than it used to be.

Pros of SaaS startups:

- High margins: SaaS startups can have an average gross margin of 65 per cent, which is very high compared to many more traditional business models.
- Scalability: Adding new features and onboarding countless users can make this type of business very scalable and profitable, often without the need for major investments.
- Build and go: A lot of SaaS startups are built and launched into the market in only a few months, once

they have enough of a product to test and see what resonates with their audience.

Cons of SaaS startups:

- Customer support: SaaS startups have users, which means great customer support is essential in order to keep them happy. That requires more day-to-day management and team-leading skills.
- Data security: SaaS startups handle a lot of sensitive data, so it is absolutely essential to be on top of the legal implications of this part of the business.
- Competition: There are countless SaaS startups out there, and most of them have competitors. It is rare to find a 'blue ocean' idea, one that is fully on its own as a new innovation without competitors.

E-commerce

E-commerce startups sit alongside SaaS in the category of most popular business models facilitated by the internet. E-commerce startups are those selling physical products online. A very different type of brand and less digital-first than everything else mentioned in this chapter, it is more of a traditional business model facilitated by the internet. The lack of a physical storefront reduces overhead costs, while allowing for global reach a lot more easily than in traditional product-based businesses. They can also be more easily scaled, starting small and then expanding their product range as they grow. Compared to traditional businesses, e-commerce businesses benefit from consumer data which allows them to understand market trends better. The internet transforms the way product-based businesses can function, by also allowing them to offer personalized customer experiences, better customer service and 24/7 availability.

Pros of e-commerce:

- Wide reach: E-commerce takes selling products many steps further, breaking physical boundaries and offering opportunities for global and constant reach.
- Marketing opportunities: Digital marketing opportunities for e-commerce brands are endless, with social media ads making it easier than ever to convert a stranger into a customer.
- Personalization and data: Compared to traditional product-first businesses, a massive benefit of e-commerce is that it provides businesses with key data on their customers' preferences and behaviours, allowing them to create products that meet their needs better.

Cons of e-commerce:

- Competition: Like many other categories in this chapter, it is very competitive. Excellent stand-out branding is essential to avoid getting lost in a huge pool of similar brands.
- Initial investment: E-commerce brands usually require a high initial investment to cover costs such as R&D, production and shipping. It is therefore less accessible than most of the other examples in this chapter, and slower to begin.

Content-based gigs

Your favourite YouTube channel, the newsletter you open most often, your top-played podcast: these are all content-based gigs, and their popularity is only increasing. With more and more ways to monetize them, they are becoming viable businesses for creators across any niche you can imagine. These are media-based jobs that often start as a passion. When someone starts creating content about something they are passionate about on social media, they often end up monetizing it and turning into a source of income. If you enjoy creating content, this could be for you. But if the term 'creating content' makes you think only of TikToks, then I'm happy to say that thankfully there are endless content-based opportunities you can try out that you might not even know are possible. On Substack, the popular social newsletter platform, writers can monetize their newsletter by offering paid subscriptions to their audience for exclusive content. They can be greatly successful as well – an analysis reported that the 27 highest-earning newsletters on Substack alone earn over $22 million per year.[12] That way, writers can make a living doing what they love, with a business model that has virtually zero running costs and is therefore very profitable. Substack is only one platform that facilitates monetizing newsletters. There are other platforms like Beehiiv, as well as many newsletters that monetize through sponsored content. Through Substack's paid subscription model, we have examples like *Noahpinion*, a newsletter primarily about economics, which has tens of thousands of paid subscribers at $10 per month. As a one-man business, it is a revolutionary way to make a great living through content creation.

I also love the type of newsletters that focus on content *curation*, such as those that send out interesting articles and links to their subscribers, or curate insightful quotes and ideas without 'creating' content from scratch. An example is *Rabbit Holes* by Patricia Mou, a newsletter that curates interesting ideas, quotes, links, essays and photos from around the internet. It takes Mou so much time to put everything together and ensure that the quality of the content always remains so high, that subscribers are happy to pay to receive it. Establishing the trust between the curator or creator and their audience is the most important thing. Once the creator can establish that they will consistently deliver high quality and remain reliable, they can monetize their content; people are happy to pay for high quality.

On the other hand, on platforms such as YouTube and on podcasts, creators usually monetize their content through ads and paid partnerships with brands. Once they have built a certain following, creators can then start working with brands in their niche, where they sponsor their content and the creators promote them in return. Brand partnerships and ads can offer a real source of income for creators, allowing them to turn their content-based gig into a full-time job. They are also often funded by using platforms like Patreon, where followers and fans pay a monthly subscription fee to receive exclusive benefits from their favourite creators. Content-based gigs are one of my favourite types of independent work specifically because they tend to start as passion projects.

I got to witness first-hand how unexpectedly well such a project can turn out, and how true it is that there are always people out there that share the same passions as you. In July 2023, a friend and I decided to start a literature podcast together. We realized that we always discussed the books we read so much, that we might as well start recording those conversations and see if anyone else reading the same books wanted to listen. We started the podcast and named it *Espresso Epilogues*, under the premise of it being two best friends talking about books over coffee. Simple and clear. Less than five months later, it had almost 18,000 TikTok followers and 210,000 monthly impressions on Spotify. The podcast has quickly become unexpectedly popular among the book community, and continues to grow organically with little effort and zero marketing spend. We started it as a fun experiment to share our mutual passion with the world, and ended up with tens of thousands of loyal listeners all around the world, before we even reached 10 episodes. That experience really showed me how well content-based gigs can work when you find a community that is equally passionate about the areas you're creating content about. Like in our case, once you validate that there is indeed demand for the content you create, there are countless avenues you can consider expanding in. From starting a Patreon or online community where your followers can support you and interact with each other, to creating adjacent businesses branching off the same brand (in our case, that could be something like a book club), content-based gigs can become entire brands with multiple streams of income.

Pros of content-based gigs:

- Passion-to-business: They often start as passion projects and turn into businesses, as social media content is a great way to showcase your passions and find potential to monetize them.
- Community: Through content-based gigs, you can build a community that loves your content and is more engaged than they would be with a typical brand.
- Free to start: Most content-based projects, like podcasts, newsletters or social media accounts, are free to start. You don't need fancy equipment, just some time to create and post.

Cons of content-based gigs:

- Constant content creation: Creating content regularly can be difficult, especially since consistency is a big part of what makes content-based projects succeed. That consistency can be hard to maintain, as it also relies on creativity and inspiration.
- Finding and building an audience: Depending on the type of business, it can be hard to find and grow an audience quickly. Consistency pays off, but it can often be a slow process, which is why many give up before getting to the stage where their content can be monetized.

Other types of independent work

These are just some examples of common types of independent work, but there are tons of people out there testing out different ways to work and carving a unique path. Dev Shah, a 22-year-old college student, is following a rare path that consists of buying and growing small companies. For two years, Dev ran his own agency helping students in India get into university. That venture allowed him to make enough money to shut down the agency and later on invest that into buying small products. Using the website Acquire.com, where users can list their products and start-ups for sale, Dev spends time finding the best deals on the platform. The first startup he bought is a product called Sourcely, an AI tool helping users find and summarize credible academic sources. He bought it for $4,000 when it was already making $500 per month, and got to scale and grow it into a successful product.

Since then, he has bought two more student-focused AI tools, and is aiming to add six more within 2024. The money from his first venture allowed him to acquire the tools he needed to turn these deals into more profitable ventures, and he is now financially secure enough to live the kind of life he wants while still at university. Rather than founding his own tools from scratch, this approach allowed Dev to focus on the things he is good at, marketing and sales, to grow products that he had already established the initial product–market fit and gone through their first stages. He also emphasized the power of posting about his business interests and activities on social media and building a personal brand: analysing businesses and posting about them on Twitter/X led to him meeting his co-founder, who handles the technical side of things, complementing his skillset. The tools he has acquired are now growing increasingly successful and without taking

Dev much time to run, as he focuses on marketing, sales, building high conversion rates with users and posting about the business scaling journey online. In order to profit from investing in startups, you used to need to have a lot more capital to spend. Today, platforms like Acquire are opening up new possibilities for entrepreneurs by making acquiring products and startups more accessible. It is an interesting way of working: it is scalable and quicker than starting multiple startups from scratch. Like Dev, entrepreneurs can end up with a suite of market-validated products that support them financially and allow them to focus on their strengths and the things they love doing. To others who want to work independently, Dev says: 'Just start small. Make sure you're doing something every week. Focus on what you can do in the next week, and do that – even if it's a small thing, just build on it week by week, iterate, and keep your goal in mind.'

Starting a project or side gig

If you take one thing from this chapter, I hope it will be that there are countless ways to make a living and work independently, no matter how young you are or what your experience is in. All of the examples mentioned show that independent work is like a tree with more branches than you can count. We tend to think of work as either this or that, either entrepreneurship or traditional work, but it is so much more complex than that, and that should be reassuring and exciting to you. It means that there are so many paths you can take, and you can always create your own.

To figure out what type of work would be best for you, first think back at whether any of the above examples really sparked your curiosity and made you want to dig deeper. If any of them caused you to imagine a certain project, then you have your starting point. Note that it is definitely better to start from a problem-first or passion-first approach, rather than a format-first approach. Instead of starting with 'maybe I'll launch a SaaS startup' or 'maybe I should try e-commerce', you should think of what problem you really want to solve, or what passion of yours you really want to pursue, and then figure out what format is best suited for that. Both a problem-first and a passion-first approach are equally valid – whatever you feel most drawn to is what you should try out, and it's even better if you can combine the two in some way. If you are passionate about writing, then a content-based gig like a newsletter or a service-based gig like copywriting (or a copywriting agency) could make sense for you. If you are passionate about climate change education, then that could lead you to creating a YouTube channel or podcast on the topic. If you are really skilled at finance and deconstructing complex topics, you could go the SaaS way and build an app helping people with financial education, or go in a completely different direction and start a newsletter deconstructing a current financial topic every week. The options are endless, the only limit is your own imagination and creativity. If you currently have a full-time job that leaves you little free time, choose a way to engage with your problem or passion that does not require a large time commitment straight away, and start little by little. I cannot stress this enough: it is much, much better to start with small steps and *put something out there*, than to wait until the 'perfect time' to give something your 100 per cent. You can give it your 100 per cent later on, but at the beginning, what you need to do is just start.

Notes

1   Zhou, L (2024) 2024 Side hustle statistics: The ultimate list, Luisa Zhou. https://www.luisazhou.com/blog/side-hustle-statistics/ (archived at https://perma.cc/6NHY-RR2S)

2   Ibid.

3   McKinsey & Company (2022) Freelance, side hustles, and gigs: Many more Americans have become independent workers, McKinsey & Company. https://www.mckinsey.com/featured-insights/sustainable-inclusive-growth/future-of-america/freelance-side-hustles-and-gigs-many-more-americans-have-become-independent-workers (archived at https://perma.cc/7MQE-R4KV)

4   MBO Partners (2022) Going, going, gone: New study reveals workers flip the script on traditional work, MBO Partners. https://www.mbopartners.com/blog/press/going-going-gone-new-study-reveals-workers-flip-the-script-on-traditional-work/ (archived at https://perma.cc/6Z8C-25DH)

5   Ibid.

6   MBO Partners (2022) Help solve the challenges of independence through talent marketplaces, MBO Partners. https://www.mbopartners.com/blog/how-grow-small-business/help-solve-the-challenges-of-independence-through-talent-marketplaces/ (archived at https://perma.cc/82KV-WJHN)

7   Shop Circle (2022) Rise of digital goods in the post-pandemic era, Shop Circle. https://shopcircle.co/blog-posts/spsc-rise-of-digital-goods-in-the-post-pandemic-era (archived at https://perma.cc/AV6D-HUTK)

8   Beckman, J (2023) Jaw-dropping 2023 online education statistics you must see, TechReport. https://techreport.com/statistics/online-education-statistics/ (archived at https://perma.cc/55P7-Q9GP)

9   Starter Story (2023) Deep Dive: 101 digital products making millions [breakdown], Starter Story. https://www.starterstory.com/stories/digital-products-making-thousands-per-month-report (archived at https://perma.cc/R35E-46D8)

10   Ingram, H (2021) I created a $1m/year subscription-based toolkit for real estate professionals, Starter Story. https://www.starterstory.com/stories/i-created-a-1m-year-subscription-based-toolkit-for-real-estate-professionals (archived at https://perma.cc/L34R-8ER7)

11   Ibid.

12   Press Gazette (2023) Revealed: Top 27 highest-earning Substack newsletters generate over $22m a year. Press Gazette. www.pressgazette.co.uk/newsletters/highest-earning-substacks/ (archived at https://perma.cc/N8WQ-8Y8X)

CHAPTER FOUR

Digital nomadism and remote work

Remote work and digital nomadism have been increasingly popular, for good reason. Whether you're working from home or travelling the world and working from anywhere, remote work presents new appealing possibilities for workers to live a freer and more exciting life. Of course, it is not for everyone. A lot of people find themselves becoming less productive when they work remotely, whether from home or while travelling or they find that one of the two ways works great for them while the other does not. At the end of this chapter, you will find a self-assessment exercise to determine how you work best, and whether this lifestyle makes sense for you. Depending on your working habits, preferences and personality, the setting in which you are your happiest and most productive self will differ. There is no one-size-fits-all for ways of working – the important thing is to find what works best for you, and create a career that allows you to work in that way.

In the past 10 years, Google searches for 'how to become a digital nomad' have almost tripled around the world. At the same time, searches for 'remote jobs' increased 1,900 per cent – this is an unprecedented change in the world of careers, and shows an incredibly significant trend that will continue to impact the future of work. The early 2000s and 2010s brought about a big rise in the digital nomad lifestyle, facilitated by the creation of digital tools like Slack that make working remotely with a team a lot easier. Co-working spaces started appearing globally to accommodate for this change, and, slowly but surely, this lifestyle became increasingly popular. But it wasn't until the Covid-19 pandemic started in 2020 that the digital nomad and remote-work lifestyles really took off. 'Work-from-home' (WFH) and 'work-from-anywhere' approaches accelerated exponentially: as people were forced to work from home and companies had to establish the necessary systems to make this possible, the world saw that remote work was more sustainable than previously thought.

Being forced to learn to work remotely on a global scale had its advantages. Remote-work-centred innovation and research skyrocketed, thousands of productivity tools and startups appeared in order to make remote work easier and more effective, and the sheer amount of research looking into the benefits of working from home or from anywhere provided important education on the topic, allowing people to make more informed choices after the pandemic.

The biggest revolution brought about by the remote-work movement is the increased emphasis on work-life balance and flexibility. We are re-evaluating the ways we work, and gaining valuable insights on how we can produce our best work and live our happiest life. Some 92 per cent of Gen Zers say the opportunity to work remotely is important to them, with 93 per cent of respondents saying they prefer hybrid or remote work over full-time office work.[1] The growing trend of flexible working is already shaping the future of work. With a push from workers demanding flexible working arrangements, many companies have had to adapt and implement more flexible arrangements. Businesses that have resisted have fallen victim to waves of resignations or employee dissatisfaction: according to Unispace,[2] 42 per cent of companies that forced a return-to-office policy had a higher level of employee dissatisfaction than expected, and 29 per cent of companies that revoked remote-work options are now struggling with recruitment.

Some were happy with the return to the office, realizing that some of the unique aspects office work offers – face-to-face meetings and working alongside colleagues for example – are necessary for them to be happy in their professional life. But for those who made large lifestyle changes as a result of this increased flexibility and became digital nomads, going back to the office seems unimaginable – it would mean giving up the opportunity to work flexibly and freely while travelling the world, to return to sitting in an office and commuting daily. Many companies do not even see a reason to have physical offices any more. In my case, The Z Link has been fully remote since day one. Born in one of the peaks of the pandemic in 2020, building it as a traditional company was not even an option for me. Having offices would be an investment that does not seem reasonable after witnessing how well we have been functioning remotely since we started. Even if it could provide extra levels of socialization and interaction among the team, companies like mine have now built their teams by hiring without borders, spread across dozens of different countries in order to be able to work with the very best talent. Giving that up for the sake of an office and in-person interaction does not seem worth it. This change in the way we work has naturally had a large socio-economic impact: demand for office spaces decreased, and more people are moving out of urban centres to prioritize locations and homes that contribute to their productivity and wellbeing.[3] According to the *Wall Street Journal*:

> the effects of the remote-work revolution are already being felt. Rents have fallen and vacancies have risen significantly in the superstar cities, particularly New York and San Francisco, according to data from Zillow and Apartment List, while smaller cities and suburbs have seen rents and home prices tick up over the past year, from Bozeman (home values up 18%) to Boise, Idaho (rents up 11%).[4]

Advantages and challenges of remote work

Whether you are trying to decide if remote work is right for you, or you are considering building a company and figuring out if it should be remote or in-person, understanding the advantages and challenges of each approach is essential. Our decision will differ based on what matters most to you in life, and what conditions and values you want to optimize for. When I interviewed 24-year-old Cameron Dower, General Manager at Legon Influence, he told me: 'In-person work is for social building, quick decision making and productive collaborative projects. Remote work is for deep, undisturbed work that requires your mind only. Both are equally important.' Understanding the benefits of both sides is important, so I won't try to sell you on the usual universal claims supporting one or the other. In my own experience, having the opportunity to work and build remotely has been life-changing, and I would not have it any other way. The benefits of being remote-first have significantly improved my life, and I am witnessing how they enable the lifestyle I feel best in. Through this chapter you may find out that this sounds like the ideal lifestyle for you too, or on the contrary, it may be that you need something different.

The biggest advantage of remote work for me has by far been the flexibility that it offers. After spending a few years trying to analyse and understand my work preferences, I have found that flexibility and freedom are core values to me – I cannot imagine being happy in a career that sacrifices those. Through remote work, I can create my own schedule and blend work and life in a way that feels healthier and more balanced. Instead of feeling like I have to work during a specific set of hours because of being in an office, I have created a daily routine that is fully aligned with the hours when I know I feel most productive. Giving myself the freedom to structure my day differently and incorporate healthy habits that contribute to my wellbeing has been a game changer. Realizing that I did not have to adhere to the schedules that I was used to in past traditional jobs was liberating, putting me in control of my day. To me, doing work that allows me to manage the structure of my day, at least to a certain extent, has become nonnegotiable. Having time to cook, go on walks, work out and take breaks when you need them is rewarding for both your professional and personal life. This is where some people disagree: remote work is often considered one of the things that harms work-life balance, because it is easy to blur the lines between life and work and end up working overtime, forgetting to check out of work and being in a state of 'always on'. If you are prone to this, it doesn't mean remote work is not for you – there are tools and methods you can use to facilitate work-life balance and draw better boundaries between the two, while benefitting from the positive parts of remote work. We will explore some of these methods later in this chapter.

Another advantage of remote work is the ability to live as a digital nomad and travel the world. A lot of young people I speak to have a goal to travel the world, and, growing up, a lot of us thought that this was something attainable much later on in one's career journey – after retiring or during the limited holidays available throughout the year. However, the increasing popularity and accessibility of the digital nomad lifestyle has shifted that mindset. Now, travelling the world is possible even at the start of one's career. As of 2023, the number of US citizens aspiring to be digital nomads or considering it for some time in the future is no fewer than 64 million.[5] With remote jobs that allow employees to work from anywhere in the world, you can get to explore different countries while having a job that supports your lifestyle. My first full-time job was like this: globally distributed team, a lot of digital nomads and systems that supported asynchronous work for efficiency even across incompatible time zones. Such companies tend to become a lot more efficient in their day-to-day operations, as they have to remove unnecessary meetings, and stick to what really is essential to enable productivity and success. I went from travelling very rarely and having visited only a couple of countries, to visiting many of my dream destinations and working from anywhere. Working for yourself can often provide you with that freedom, but even if you are not entrepreneurial, there are jobs out there (most commonly at startups) that allow this type of lifestyle. Travelling the world can expand your mindset and community and expose you to opportunities and people that are incredibly hard to access otherwise. It is an experience unlike any other, and which can be one of the most rewarding things you will ever do. If travelling the world is one of your goals and passions, then structuring your career in a way that supports remote work should be a priority.

Perhaps our most precious resource is time – and the future of work largely favours remote work because it allows us to control our time in a way that is mostly unprecedented in traditional career structures. In 2021 and 2022, it was measured that working from home saved the average worker about two hours per week.[6] This time tends to go primarily towards secondary jobs and other work (such as using the extra hours to build a side gig or explore new avenues), and secondly towards leisure.[7] As a result of this extra time and flexibility, mental health and productivity have reportedly improved for many remote workers, with 86 per cent of them stating that remote work has reduced their stress and improved their well-being.[8] To me, one of the goals of designing a career on my terms is exactly that: making sure that my work is facilitating my wellbeing and happiness instead of constantly stressing me out. We are so used to work being stressful by default, that we forget there are other ways to be. When I find my work increasingly stressing me out and disrupting my peace of mind every day, which of course happens, I take it as a sign that it is time to make a change. I evaluate whether I can let go of a specific project or responsibility that seems to be taking more of a toll on me instead of contributing positively to my work somehow. This way of operating allows me to remain in touch with how my work is affecting me every day, and whether what I am spending my time on is good for me. Remote work is one of the things that have helped me optimize for that, by giving me control of my time.

Of course, remote work comes with a few challenges, but most of them are nothing you can't find solutions for. The first one is regarding digital nomadism – while it is a lifestyle many aspire towards and it is becoming increasingly accessible, it is not equally accessible to everyone globally. Visa and tax obligations can be difficult to figure out, and are harder for some countries than others. For example, establishing tax residency as a digital nomad is difficult: some countries use the '183-day rule' to determine whether someone has become a tax resident, but it is not the only factor they consider. Local bank accounts, property ownership and other elements play a role as well. Nomads often have to plan their travel around that, ensuring they stay on top of their visa and tax obligations so legal challenges do not catch up with them later. Tax laws are very complicated and so far there is no single authority making that easy for digital nomads to navigate. For example, someone living in one country but working for a company based in another country could face tax obligations in both locations, so it is important to always be on top of each country's requirements to ensure compliance. Of course, that can be exhausting and resource-intensive, as it can require consultations with lawyers or accountants. It is perhaps the most tangibly difficult part of being a digital nomad, and hopefully we will see more tools and resources in the next few years dedicated to supporting nomads in this area. While many countries now offer digital nomad visas, their requirements are not uniform, so it is not straightforward to plan moves between different countries. Figuring out where you are allowed to work from and what that means legally and tax-wise is a complicated and time-consuming process, so the digital nomad lifestyle requires careful planning in order to be sustainable. Luca Mussari, co-founder at Freaking Nomads, puts it best:

The reality of taxation for digital nomads is far from straightforward. In fact, it's a gray area that often leaves digital nomads navigating a labyrinth of outdated laws and regulations that haven't quite caught up with the modern reality of remote work. Let's consider a hypothetical scenario: Marco, a digital nomad from Italy, decides to deregister as a resident in his home country and fly to Bali to live and work. He assumes that by doing this, he's free from the obligation of paying taxes in Italy. However, this is a common misconception and is mostly incorrect. Many developed countries, including Italy, have in fact what's known as a tax residency fallback principle. This principle essentially means that if you're not a tax resident in another country, you're automatically considered a tax resident in the last country where you were a resident. So, in Marco's case, unless he becomes a tax resident of Indonesia (or another country), he would still be considered an Italian tax resident for tax purposes! This is just one example of the many complex tax laws that digital nomads need to navigate.[9]

Another issue is the isolation that can arise from working remotely, whether from home or as a digital nomad. With constant moving or the lack of a physical office, it is easy to lose the community you would have in a traditional career. Remote work does not facilitate socializing and building community like in-person work does, and that is an issue many struggle with. Meeting people and socializing has to become a more conscious effort, while those working in an office are used to it coming to them effortlessly as a part of daily life. If you switch from a traditional career to one that is remote or nomadic, there are many things you can do to maintain a community around you and build a healthy social life. If you are working from home, minus the travel, it is a bit easier. You just need to go about maintaining a community around you more intentionally: not relying on work to see friends, but instead actively seeking out the people you want to be spending time with, whether that's by joining clubs or reconnecting with old friends. If you are working in a remote team, there is often still an element of community that companies make an effort to maintain: virtual socials, occasional retreats and opportunities to get to know your colleagues better since you don't get to experience that in-person. But if you are working for yourself, that aspect of meeting people through work does not exist in quite the same way. However, there are so many ways to facilitate that. Let's look at some of the best ways to build a community as a remote worker.

Building a remote work community

There are online communities of all kinds that allow independent workers to meet others on similar journeys, communities focused on personal and professional networking, as well as in-person communities that organize meetups in cities around the world specifically so those on independent career paths can meet others like them. We live in a good time to be working independently or remotely, with so many tools to support each aspect of that lifestyle and make the experience as rewarding as possible. For digital nomads, there is an even stronger sense of community around the world: there are countless online and in-person communities focused on the digital nomad lifestyle. Cities that have become big nomad hubs, such as Chiang Mai in Thailand or Lisbon in Portugal, provide tons of opportunities for socialization, and nomads working from there will find constant meetups, retreats and events specifically for them. Almost every nomad hub has Facebook groups and online communities you can easily find which make it very straightforward to meet new people and network. This aspect of nomad life makes it a type of work that often provides even *more* opportunities for socialization than traditional work, specifically because the nomad community worldwide is so active in that domain. Co-working spaces are also a great way to get the benefits of in-person work while maintaining the freedom to work remotely and build your own schedule however you want. Whether you work from different countries or you are stable and working from home, co-working spaces solve a lot of the common remote work problems: connectivity issues, lack of community, finding it hard to focus at home/while travelling. There are companies like Selina CoWork that provide spaces around the world designed primarily for digital nomads, remote workers and travellers. They offer spaces for accommodation, co-working and socializing all in one, with many locations across the world. They are popular among travellers who seek co-working and co-living experiences with fellow remote workers and digital nomads, as this is one of the best ways to meet like-minded people and make the remote work experience a lot more enjoyable. There are more such businesses that focus on elevating the remote work lifestyle and solving the isolation problem, to the point where once you become aware of it, there are solutions everywhere. In my experience, letting this challenge dissuade you from pursuing a remote or nomadic lifestyle is not worth it – more and more communities are popping up, even in cities that are not traditional nomad hubs. The global community of nomads and remote workers is becoming increasingly connected and the original issue of isolation has been replaced with a benefit – that of finding a rewarding and enriching global community.

How to successfully work remotely

Remote work requires a lot of different skills: time management, great communication, discipline and self-drive among others. If you want to work remotely and benefit from all the advantages of that lifestyle, there are many areas to focus on to ensure that your remote work experience is successful, rather than stressful and unproductive. Time management is an essential area that you need to master. Luckily, there is no shortage of resources and tools to help you manage your time efficiently. When I was at university, time management had to become my strength: I was juggling full-time classes with building and running my business, as well as a full-time remote job and extracurricular activities I was involved in at university. And somehow, I still managed to get eight hours of sleep. Figuring out how to do that took some trial and error, and I gained some lessons that can hopefully help you as well, no matter how many things you currently have on your plate. Remote work presents a lot of unique time-management challenges by blending work and life in a way that can be hard to fight against. I've tried various popular time-management and productivity tips and many of them didn't work for me. Just because something works for someone else (or millions of people), does not mean it will work for you too. For example, the Pomodoro technique (25 minutes of work followed by five-minute breaks) never clicked with me – it didn't feel like it was contributing to my productivity levels; it just felt forced. The same happened each time I tried to use software that overcomplicated to-do lists and tasks. Organization is great, but too much organization can simply become counter productive. You need to experiment and create your own system, committing yourself to the techniques that have a positive impact on your productivity and output. If you are trying to manage your time as a remote worker, here are some ideas I would recommend:

- Experiment with different time-management methods and tools to see if any of them actually help you. I like one called Llama Life, which combines time management with task management.
- Time blocking: blocking out time on your calendar for everything you need to get done in a day, and sticking to that. This worked for me during incredibly busy times, but beyond that, it proved to be too stressful for me to plan out my day so strictly. But if you are someone who thrives on strict planning, time blocking could skyrocket your productivity.
- Look at your to-do list and estimate how long each task will take. This helps me during especially busy periods.

You can then prioritize by starting with all the small tasks (10 minutes or less) and just the act of getting them out of the way early in the day makes everything feel more manageable.

There are many ways to prioritize and manage your tasks, so the best thing you can do is experiment with a few different approaches and work out what elevates (rather than hinders) your productivity levels.

The topic of productivity goes beyond time management – when you work remotely, your productivity is in your hands more than in traditional jobs. This can be a challenge or an opportunity. The first thing you need to do is set clear boundaries with yourself and with others. You'd be surprised at how many remote workers do not have clear boundaries with themselves around what times they work, and how they operate when they are in non-work mode. Set specific working hours and communicate them with your team, family, friends or roommates, so that there are clear expectations around when you are available and when you are 'at work'. When you set your own boundaries and stick to them, you are much more likely to have a productive remote-work experience because the borders between work and life are clearly defined. The same goes with having a dedicated space where you work; working and living in the same spaces makes it harder to mentally check out of work at the end of the day, so if you work and sleep in the same room, you might find yourself being constantly under stress. Work-from-home experts that spoke to CNBC stated that it's important to create a separate space for work at home: Pam Cohen, a research scientist who has been studying remote work for 20 years, advises that if you're working from home and don't have the ability to move to a separate room or co-working space, then you can use smaller physical cues to help your brain switch on and off work, for example by setting up your laptop in the morning and hiding it out of sight in the evening.[10] This helps your brain focus and get into work mode every time you are at your dedicated workspace or when you see your laptop, and you can switch off when you want personal time.

I also love using apps and tools to limit distractions, as getting easily distracted is a constant challenge in remote work. It is so easy to fall into distractions that appear from every side without realizing it. This becomes even harder when you work in social media, where the lines between professional and personal use can disappear very easily. To help yourself stay productive, use tools that block these distractions when you ask them to, and you will notice your focus levels improving drastically. Now that I have been working remotely for years, I cannot remember how I ever lived without my phone and laptop on 'do not disturb' mode. Getting notified by every single email you receive is just unnecessary – if anything, you can set specific times in your workday where you check work-related notifications, or create filters so the ones that are usually time-sensitive stay on. By default, social media apps send you notifications that have nothing to do with you: Twitter/X sends post recommendations it thinks you might like; Instagram sends notifications just to say that a few people recently posted on their stories. Of course they do – they are built to grab your attention whenever they lose it, and pull you back into using the apps. But just because they are built like that, doesn't mean we can't make the experience healthier for ourselves. My productivity and focus levels improved, and my stress levels decreased so much, since I stopped allowing these apps to send me endless notifications. Depending on your device, you can use focus modes to limit notifications during a certain time. iPhones allow you to create custom focus filters, so you can have one for sleep, one for deep work and so on. I even have one called 'personal' which is on 24/7, which only allows the apps I use to speak with friends and family, and some specific work apps. Everything else, like email, random app notifications and most social media notifications, only show up when I check them manually. If you rely on social media apps for your work, another option may be customizing your notifications in your settings – allowing notifications for direct messages while blocking 'recommendation' notifications, for example.

This creates a digital work-life separation when you don't have the physical distinction created by commuting to and from an office. The same can be done on your laptop, and there are apps that take it one step further. Browser extensions like Stay Focusd allow you to block distracting websites, and there are tons of other tools that will go as far as hiding all the content from social media websites and distracting apps if you end up there, so your feed will appear fully empty. There are also paid apps like Freedom that work across all your devices and allow you to control what distractions they block, putting you in control of what you see. If you are prone to distractions (and these days, who isn't?), trying one of these solutions can make a massive difference in your focus, stress and productivity.

I also find that when you work remotely, it is even more important to set a specific routine – you cannot be truly productive if work is the only area of your life going well, because eventually you will burn out. The key is to always find ways to focus on different areas of your life, to strike a balance. Remote work is a huge challenge which, with some discipline, you can turn into an incredible opportunity, which is one of the things I love the most about it. Besides giving you freedom when it comes to work, it grants you freedom in other parts of your life.

Adele Bloch, a 25-year-old product manager and founder, told me that she used remote work to travel with her friends exploring various parts of the US West Coast while working. Moving between different states and Airbnbs, they got to work during the day, and hike, explore and see nature in the evenings.

> We were living such a fulfilling lifestyle – working remotely during the day, and adventuring at night. We focused a lot on enjoying the outdoors. Some example post-work outings: hiking at Zion National Park in Utah, floating down the Deschutes River in Bend, jumping into a 32-degree natural pool in Oregon and watching the sunset over the ocean in Seattle. It was definitely a once-in-a-lifetime opportunity that we're forever grateful for.

Your life can become completely different thanks to remote work: you can go from work taking up the largest part of your everyday life, to it helping you rebalance the different areas of your life to feel more fulfilled. To achieve that, discipline plays a big role. After setting boundaries and times to define when you are working and when you're not, it is practically your time to shine – that is, assuming your working hours are somewhat flexible. After I made an effort to become more aware of the habits and activities that help me feel the happiest and healthiest every day, I realized that jumping into work mode first thing when I wake up is simply something that does not work for me. Instead, I pushed my working hours to later in the day, and started taking a couple of hours every morning to start the day with activities that contribute to my peace of mind and wellness: meditating, going to exercise classes, taking my time to eat a good breakfast and overall making a very conscious effort to not feel rushed in the morning. And then, I start working once I feel like my mind is in the right place. I experimented with so many different routines and just found that I had a lot of mental blocks and false beliefs about what work had to look like. I thought that if I was taking hours in the morning to focus on myself first, I was somehow not being productive.

We all have so many mental blocks around what work is 'supposed' to look like, and recognizing them is liberating because you realize that there is no single way you are meant to work. Your life is yours to live, and only you know when you feel like your best self – so creating a flexible work structure can allow you to implement that every day. After the initial excitement of my 'wow, now I work remotely so I can travel the world' phase, I also realized that travelling all the time while I was working was not the best for my productivity. Especially during short trips, changing scenery, adjusting and managing to get into a rhythm of work and productivity while in a new place just wasn't working for me (although for a lot of people, it's the best way to work!). During long trips, I was just too prone to distractions, so my work would come in bursts of focus and productivity without any consistency. The idea of travelling to a different country and working in the process sounded perfect in theory, but after a few experiments, I just saw that I would end up sitting at a cafe doing maybe one or two hours of meaningful work, without the ability to actually focus for longer. What works is either working from the city I am based in and taking time off while travelling, or travelling for much longer periods to actually experience a more nomadic lifestyle. If you spend at least a couple of weeks in a new place and get to adjust and experience it like a local, the nomadic lifestyle becomes a lot more rewarding and brings you the consistency that is otherwise hard to find. This might be the same for you, as a lot of nomads find that it is when they have the time to settle in and establish a routine in a new place that they can actually be productive and experience the best this lifestyle has to offer. Switching cities or countries every week rarely works as well as we expect it to – so if you are considering a nomadic lifestyle, that is my best advice.

Life as a digital nomad

Even at the very start of your career, you can reach your goals and create the career you dream of as a digital nomad if that is the lifestyle you want to follow. Leo Ariel is a 23-year-old writer and ex-software engineer who quit his corporate job to start travelling the world and working remotely. In January 2023, while at a digital nomad event in Argentina, he met someone who would become his best friend and co-founder. This is one of the best things about the nomad community around the world – so many people are open to collaboration and keen to meet like-minded people, so you never know how it may lead to new opportunities. Exposing yourself to that community as a nomad and going out of your way to attend digital nomad events and interact with others can change your life, as it did in Leo's case. As a result, he got to build a company remotely while travelling the world, with him and his co-founder sometimes collaborating from opposite sides of the world. As both of them are travel lovers, building a company remotely just made sense. 'This whole idea that you can build a company from different parts of the world was crazy to me; if you told me before a year ago, I wouldn't have believed you. I learned so much from the experience, and I highly recommend to young people curious about entrepreneurship to try it.' The range of people you will meet and opportunities you will expose yourself to as a digital nomad are almost impossible to arise in a traditional work setting. If I were just starting out with a digital nomad life, the following are some resources, tools and places I would look for inspiration and information.

First, as the digital nomad community is so active and people love educating others on the ins and outs of this lifestyle, there is no shortage of blogs and websites by successful digital nomads you can check out. If you are looking for resources and insights on the digital nomad lifestyle, there are many experts out there sharing the digital nomad experience and providing toolkits, travel guides and more. Here are a few I would recommend:

- Nomadic Matt: Having travelled to over 100 countries, his website provides content on how to travel on a budget, nomad tips and in-depth travel guides for dozens of countries with all the details you need to know. His travel guides include typical costs, suggested budgets and money-saving tips, so you can easily navigate the often mysterious part of how much it would cost to live in a specific country.
- Expert Vagabond: His website provides information on jobs that pay to travel the world, as well as transparent information on how he funds his nomad lifestyle, and guidance on starting a travel blog that can be monetized.
- Remote OK: A website that lists jobs that are remote and allow you to work from anywhere. If you are not convinced that working for yourself is right for you, you can still build a flexible career on your terms by being employed remotely.
- *How to Be a Digital Nomad* by Kayla Ihrig: A practical guide to digital nomadism, which includes tips on making and saving money abroad, preparing to travel, deciding where to go and insight into how to take control of your career while travelling the world.
- A Little Adrift: A blog by Shannon O'Donnell, who was named Traveller of the Year by National Geographic in 2013 and has travelled to over 100 countries since 2008. Her website focuses on how nomads can connect to the culture of the places they visit, practical advice for

planning long-term travel, and sharing tools and resources for living and working abroad.

The appeal of office life

There is a reason that 68 per cent of Gen Zers surveyed across 40 countries stated that hybrid work is their preferred way of working, compared to 24 per cent that said they prefer fully remote.[11] Office life has some unique benefits that a lot of Gen Zers have not been able to experience due to entering the job market at a time of increased remote work post-pandemic. For many, the traditional routine of going to the office to work has a lot of advantages that are not easy to replicate in a remote work setting.

Paul Scherer, a Gen Z entrepreneur and marketer, says that even though most of his jobs have been remote, if he were to build a company today, he would make it an in-person company with an office. He considers going to the office to be a cultural advantage, especially for early-stage startups: 'Organizations that are in-office tend to be a lot more aligned. You don't need as many processes, because people naturally talk to each other. There's better communication when everyone is in the same time zone, because you're all on the same page, and things are communicated more efficiently.' This is backed up by a large study conducted with over 61,000 Microsoft employees, which found that asynchronous communication due to remote work may have made it more difficult for teams to collaborate and convey complex information.[12] One suggestion that came from these results is that this type of impact on collaboration and effective communication may, in the long term, hinder productivity and even innovation. It is likely, then, that office-based work can provide a different way of collaborating and communicating, which is not only beneficial for business but also for employees to do more effective work.

Another advantage is the relationship-building and socializing aspect that is tied to office-based work. Especially at the start of one's career, having the ability to easily meet people and connect with co-workers in an office setting can be very rewarding. Research shows that almost 100 per cent of employees believe that in-person meetings build strong long-term relationships.[13] Being able to build a strong network can then contribute to your future career prospects, open new doors and present opportunities that may have otherwise been inaccessible. It also provides a socialization aspect that can make work more fun and engaging compared to the potential isolation of working remotely – if you like the people you work with, getting to work, collaborating and socializing with them in person can be a very rewarding addition to your daily life. This can also foster a greater sense of belonging: if you are part of a team, getting to engage with it in person usually makes you feel a lot more involved and invested in it.

Traditional office-based environments, then, help create a real separation between work and life, the issue that a lot of remote workers struggle with. When the routine of going into the office is set, the boundaries between work and life are a lot clearer. You get to have a set place and time where you engage with work, making it easier to disconnect when you get home. Not everyone can create an efficient and productive routine while working from home, as creating that boundary and maintaining work-life balance is definitely a challenging task. For Gen Zers entering the job market and just learning how to navigate work-life balance, office work can make that process easier. Finally, office work allows for more direct feedback, which contributes to professional and personal growth. Learning from your work is essential, and office-based jobs make it easier for managers and peers to offer immediate feedback and facilitate those conversations that lead to development. It is clear that office-based work offers a lot of benefits that you might want to take advantage of at some point in your career. For Gen Z, it seems to be a balance of getting the best of both worlds – either finding hybrid work so they have the option to choose between remote and in-person, or trialling traditional office jobs for a while, and then switching to remote.

Self-evaluation

You now know how to go about creating a successful lifestyle as a remote worker or digital nomad, but if you have never tried it, how can you know if that's what you want? Doubts about making such a leap and regretting it for some reason are normal – it is a big life change, and can be a big career pivot too. To help you assess whether remote work or digital nomadism would work well for you, there are some specific questions you can answer that will uncover your work preferences and personality traits which might make remote work a good or not-so-good fit. After digging deep into successful remote work and nomad stories, I drew some criteria that seem to be the most essential for a successful remote career: adaptability, self-discipline, communication, comfort with technology, financial management, openness and more. There are 20 questions. For each one, answer honestly with a 'Yes' or 'No'. Don't overthink it too much, sometimes your intuitive answers are the best ones. At the end of the exercise, you will get to measure and understand what your answers mean. If you are reading a physical copy of this book, go ahead and annotate it to make the exercise easier. Here we go (*be honest!*):

1 Do you tend to adapt easily to new environments and situations?
2 Are you comfortable with frequent changes to your daily routine?
3 Can you stay productive without someone directly supervising you?
4 Do you feel like you can stay motivated and driven without someone pushing you or holding you accountable?
5 Do you have a history of meeting deadlines and achieving goals independently?
6 Are you comfortable communicating mainly online (emails, messaging apps, video calls)?
7 Do you feel comfortable expressing your needs in a remote setting, like in a meeting or through chat?
8 Are you comfortable using various digital tools and platforms for work?

9 Do you pick up new technologies or software quickly?

10 Can you maintain a healthy work-life balance when working from home or while travelling?

11 Do you stick to the boundaries you set between work and personal time?

12 Are you comfortable managing your finances and budgeting?

13 Are you comfortable meeting new people in new settings, like events, travel or networking occasions?

14 Are you generally comfortable with managing periods of solitude without feeling lonely or isolated?

15 Do you enjoy experiencing new cultures and interacting with people from diverse backgrounds?

16 Do you feel comfortable with different local customs when travelling (instead of them putting you off or making you uncomfortable)?

17 When unexpected challenges arise, are you usually calm rather than panicked?

18 Do you feel comfortable seeking solutions when problems arise rather than waiting for guidance?

19 Are you good at staying in touch with people you don't see often?

20 Are you good at self-care and stress management during busy periods?

Time to evaluate your answers! First, count how many 'Yes' answers you had. Here is what they mean:

13–20 'Yes' answers: Digital nomadism and remote work are perfectly suited lifestyles for you! Whether you choose to travel or work from home, you're equipped with most of the things that are needed to make remote work, work.

10–12 'Yes' answers: You seem to have a lot of the traits that make someone well-suited for a remote work or digital nomad lifestyle. You have the qualities and mindset that would help you thrive in such an environment. Take note of the areas where you are lacking, and consider how you can work on them to enhance your experience even further.

7–9 'Yes' answers: You might enjoy remote work or digital nomadism, but there are areas to improve on to ensure you have a good experience. What do the questions for which you answered 'No' tell you about areas where you can improve? Try to notice the underlying patterns and see if you can focus on developing those skills or mindset.

Fewer than 7 'Yes' answers: Even if you would enjoy remote work or digital nomadism, you would likely find it challenging. Consider whether something in the middle might work better for you, like hybrid work or travelling only when you are not working.

But don't forget: there are no skills you cannot develop, so this assessment is merely an overview of where you stand at this moment in time. Growth mindset, which I mentioned in previous chapters, applies here too – if this is something you want to do, developing new skills or working on your mindset could be a great challenge to embark on for personal and professional growth. This exercise is just a guide to help you reflect on how ready you are at this moment for remote work or a nomadic lifestyle. Hopefully, the resources, tools and tips in this chapter have helped you gain a better understanding of what a life of remote work or nomadism is like, what you can gain from it and how to solve the potential challenges that most remote workers have to deal with. In my experience, remote work and digital nomadism can be liberating experiences that really stretch the bounds of what your life can look like; that is why a lot of independent workers focus on creating location-independent careers, and now you know the first steps you can take to do the same.

Notes

1   The Z Link (2023) Gen Z + Careers, The Z Link. www.thezlink.com/research/careers (archived at https://perma.cc/7DKQ-ZC9V)
2   Tsipursky, G (2023) We're now finding out the damaging results of the mandated return to the office–and it's worse than we thought, Fortune Europe. https://fortune.com/europe/2023/08/01/research-damaging-results-mandated-return-to-office-worse-than-we-thought-rto-remote-work-careers-leadership-gleb-tsipursky/ (archived at https://perma.cc/G35Q-8L6F)
3   Florida, R. (2021) How remote work is reshaping America's urban geography, The Wall Street Journal. https://www.wsj.com/articles/how-remote-work-is-reshaping-americas-urban-geography-11614960100 (archived at https://perma.cc/7LFD-LZV7)
4   Ibid.
5   Aksoy, C G, Barrero, J M, Bloom, N, Davis, S, Dolls, M and Zarate, P (2023) Commute time savings when working from home, VoxEU.org (archived at https://perma.cc/DFG5-PKJH), 24 January. https://cepr.org/voxeu/columns/commute-time-savings-when-working-home (archived at https://perma.cc/7JGX-DX2S)
6   Ibid.
7   Ibid.

8 Clark, S (2022) Remote work statistics: 15 stats you need to know in 2022, Krisp Blog, 10 August. https://krisp.ai/blog/remote-working-statistics/ (archived at https://perma.cc/XF9V-MTAK)

9 Mussari, L (2024) Digital nomad taxes: Your guide to legally travel and work remotely, Freaking Nomads. https://freakingnomads.com/taxes-for-digital-nomads/ (archived at https://perma.cc/M3V9-6YYN)

10 Liu, J (2020) When work and home are the same place, experts say this is how to find balance, CNBC. https://www.cnbc.com/2020/03/27/when-work-and-home-are-the-same-place-this-is-how-to-find-balance.html (archived at https://perma.cc/3S7R-6ZHH)

11 The Z Link (2023) Gen Z + Careers, The Z Link. www.thezlink.com/research/careers (archived at https://perma.cc/7DKQ-ZC9V)

12 Yang, L, Holtz, D, Jaffe, S, Suri, S, Sinha, S, Weston, J, Joyce, C, Shah, N, Sherman, K, Hecht, B and Teevan, J (2022) The effects of remote work on collaboration among information workers, Nature Human Behaviour, 6, 43–54

13 Teamstage (2022) Networking statistics: General stats, benefits, face to face, and more! Teamstage Blog. https://teamstage.io/networking-statistics/ (archived at https://perma.cc/ZUR9-HXKG)

CHAPTER FIVE

Personal branding

The importance of personal branding

Imagine if your next boss didn't have to read your résumé because he already reads your blog. Imagine being a student and getting your first gig based on a school project you posted online. Imagine losing your job but having a social network of people familiar with your work and ready to help you find a new one. Imagine turning a side project or a hobby into your profession because you had a following that could support you. All you have to do is show your work.

AUSTIN KLEON, *SHOW YOUR WORK!*

This is what personal branding is all about.

In our digital economy, personal branding has quickly become one of the main factors that can influence one's success. A strong personal brand can push you forward and bring about opportunities that would otherwise never have found you. The lack of a personal brand can result in you getting lost in a sea of similarly qualified ambitious people, where the ones that are most public about what they do will inevitably stand out. That is what personal branding is about: just as we brand companies and products to make them stand out in their industry, also 'branding' ourselves online can help differentiate us. Personal branding is the story you tell about yourself online. It is the act of intentionally crafting the associations that people will have about you when they hear your name. For example, if you are very passionate about sustainability and want to attract opportunities and connections in the field, you should centre your personal brand around that topic. By consistently sharing insights and thoughts about it on your social media, you create this association in your followers' minds. When they stumble upon sustainability-related opportunities, you will come to mind. In contrast, if no one besides the people close to you knows what you are passionate about or interested in pursuing, the barrier between you and exciting opportunities will be much higher. Building a personal brand also expands your network: in addition to showing the people who know and follow you what you want to be associated with, one of the most impactful effects of personal branding is that you attract new people who would not have found you otherwise.

There is also a lot of data to support investing time and effort into personal branding. According to research by

Forbes, 90 per cent of recruiters say they conduct online research on potential candidates.[1] That means that your social media will likely be seen by a potential recruiter and, if you are posting on LinkedIn about your area of interest, you can appear as an active voice in the field. According to Brand Builders, 63 per cent of Americans are likely to buy from a person who has a strong personal brand.[2] So if you are selling a service or product, it is much more likely to appeal to your target audience if your own personal brand seems trustworthy. *Entrepreneur* magazine also found that 92 per cent of people trust the recommendations of individuals over companies.[3] So if you are thinking of starting a business, it is essential to consider how your personal brand as a founder will lead people to your company, rather than thinking only about how the company can market itself.

I started being active on Twitter/X on the topics of entrepreneurship and marketing around 2020, when I launched my company. I began slowly, without going about it too intentionally at that point; but over time, as I learned and shared my insights, followed relevant people and engaged with them, I built an audience of thousands that were all interested in the same things. I ended up meeting dozens, if not hundreds, of young entrepreneurs through that. It became an invaluable part of my business's growth and success. Aside from attracting new clients, I was hired as Head of Social Media at a Series-A startup based in San Francisco as a result of my Twitter/X presence. It allowed me to work fully remotely while I was still at university and build my own startup, while having a salary better than anything I could have imagined at that point. It offered me full financial freedom so I could invest most of the salary into my own company. I was 21 years old when that happened, and it directly influenced my ability to scale my company without having to worry about profitability from day one. With flexible hours and location independence, it was the perfect scenario. It taught me a lot about what a full-time job can be like, and what it does not have to be like. None of that would have happened had I not been active on Twitter/X. I did not apply for that job. They found me in a Slack community and reached out, looking for a young social media specialist. Once hired I was told that they were looking for someone that seemed like they 'get' social media which, in the startup world, tends to be a lot about Twitter/X and your style of writing.

There is a concept called 'conditions for emergence' – it refers to the fact that if you want something to happen, but you cannot force it, you have to create the conditions for it to emerge. You cannot fall asleep on command, but you can create the conditions for sleep: turning off the lights, not looking at your phone before bed and so on. Building your personal brand is about creating the conditions for success and opportunities, through visibility, networking, associations and credibility.

Credibility is a key factor in why building a personal brand is important. Aside from becoming visible in your field, you become more credible and trustworthy. It often goes like this: a hiring manager has two candidates for a design role. Candidate A posts actively on social media about design trends and showcases their work, while Candidate B does not. Even if Candidate B is technically more experienced or has more years of design work under their belt, Candidate A appears more credible thanks to their personal branding. Creating content online is a great way to showcase your expertise or passion about a topic, in a way that people can immediately grasp and trust. You will be viewed as a leader in the field, or at least as someone who has made the active effort to get involved, more than they have to. Once you are making progress in your career, maintaining your personal brand is what will help you continue to stand out, attract opportunities and establish yourself as an authority in your field. Most of my speaking opportunities at conferences and panels around the world have been a result of me posting on LinkedIn. Each platform has its benefits if you use it right. It just so happens that a lot of conferences search on LinkedIn to find experts in a field, and if you post consistently, you are far easier to find.

Strategies for building your personal brand

Personal branding is not just about creating content around your chosen topic or industry. It is also about understanding what makes you unique, and seeing how you can offer value to an audience through that. I am a firm believer that we can learn something from anyone, and that includes you. You are a collection of unique experiences and influences. The skills you have cultivated throughout your life, the talents and passions that always came naturally to you, your personal projects, your hobbies, the books you have read... The accumulation of all of these different facets of who you are makes you special. Personal branding is about recognizing your strengths and building on them, instead of going against them. If you have always been an avid reader, for example, and you want to build your personal brand around the mental health field, part of your content strategy could revolve around sharing insights from relevant books in a digestible and consistent way. Take some time to reflect on your personal strengths and the skills that always came easily to you. Investor and entrepreneur Naval Ravikant speaks of the concept of 'specific knowledge', which can help you identify where your uniqueness lies:

> Figure out what you were doing as a kid or teenager almost effortlessly. Something you didn't even consider a skill, but people around you noticed. Your mother or your best friend growing up would know. Examples of what your specific knowledge could be:
>
> - Sales skills
> - Musical talents, with the ability to pick up any instrument
> - An obsessive personality: you dive into things and remember them quickly
> - Love for science fiction, which means you absorb a lot of knowledge very quickly
> - Playing a lot of games, you understand game theory pretty well.
>
> The specific knowledge is a weird combination of unique traits from your DNA, your unique upbringing and your response to it. It's almost baked into your personality and your identity. Then you can hone it.

Underneath your passions and your natural abilities are deeper skills that can help you figure out important parts of your personality that you can leverage. A lot of people never stop to wonder what their innate abilities are and how they can leverage them in a way that does not feel like work. Think about what feels easy and enjoyable to you but hard and laborious to others. That's what you need to optimize. While it's important to continue developing new skills, I believe that everyone has at least one key strength that they can leverage without much strain. Combined with the will to learn new skills, this can make you irreplaceable. Mine, for example, is the ability to deliver things quickly, to work efficiently without overthinking. What is your strength, and how can it help you create value? This might be a question you think about for a long time. It is not necessary to have all the answers, but keeping it in mind will steer you in the right direction while focusing on your personal brand.

This chapter will dive into actionable strategies to start building your personal brand on social media, so that you can go ahead and implement some of these tips straight away. You will also learn from some Gen Zers that are mastering personal branding, and leave with recommended resources you can look into to take your skills to a new level. The first important issue to figure out is which social media platforms you should be active on (aside from what you do for personal use). Every platform is different, and some of them have their own unofficial micro-communities that you can become a part of when you post and engage with others. Twitter/X has a very strong community around entrepreneurship and venture capital, for example. LinkedIn has a very active marketing community, where young professionals constantly go viral for posting about latest marketing campaigns, trends and industry news, thus building a like-minded audience. TikTok can also be incredibly helpful for some industries. Those in more visual fields, like design, can thrive on TikTok. Whether by redesigning popular brand identities or showcasing interesting trends, they can tap into the strong design community of the platform and establish themselves as an active member. So how do you choose where to focus your efforts? First, take some time to do an industry deep-dive and explore those who have the most prominent personal brands in your field. Your personal strengths also come into play here: if you love video editing or communicating visually, you could stand out on TikTok, while if you are a natural writer, Twitter/X could be better for you.

Improving engagement

Social media is inherently... well, social. It is easy to forget this and focus all our time on creating as much content as possible, posting a lot, and waiting for the right people and opportunities to find us. But an essential part of your personal brand strategy is engaging with other people. It is a two-way conversation: if you only post into the void, you will not be able to grow as easily or quickly. That goes for every social media platform. When you determine which platforms you would like to focus on, spend some time regularly following people with similar interests and commenting on a few posts. On TikTok and Twitter/X, everyone engages very casually. You do not have to come up with something to say just for the sake of engagement, but rather you can focus on your natural reaction to a post and simply engage with people around it. Twitter/X, especially, is all about conversation. This is the best way to get on someone's radar (like someone from your industry you would like to connect with, a potential client or mentor) in a way that is genuine and not spammy. LinkedIn is full of people who comment just for the sake of commenting. The rise of AI triggered a collection of tools that comment on posts for you, but in a way that, let's face it, sounds quite unnatural. Their selling point is helping you engage more actively with people in your industry and thus giving your profile more exposure, but it is becoming increasingly rare to see genuine comments in an ocean of AI-generated ones that simply rephrase the original post in the premise of agreeing. When you find someone on LinkedIn that you would like to engage with, it is better to send them a personalized message referencing their work or their content, in a way that can lead to valuable conversation or even a call. It is a great way to expand your network and get to know people you can learn from. Engaging with others on social media is a vital aspect of building your personal brand, as long as you do it mindfully and with the intention of being genuine. Do not spam anyone or comment asking for people to follow you back, it will only achieve the opposite effect.

One of my favourite ways to use my personal brand for engagement is getting organic PR. As a business owner, being featured in the press has brought me endless opportunities. Contrary to how many people believe the press works, I have never paid for any type of press feature. It has all been organic, and easier than you would expect

– it's a hidden life hack! When I first started The Z Link, I wanted to get it featured *somewhere*, anywhere. I was sure the demand was there and our offering would resonate with people, I just needed to get it in front of a niche audience, ideally without running paid ads, as I had zero budget at the time. I did some research and found journalists who wrote about social media marketing and Gen Z in various publications, and reached out to them via Twitter/X DM. An essential part of making this work is knowing how to talk to people without making it a one-sided ask. When you message a journalist asking them to write about you and your business, especially if you follow up later, you just end up looking like another spam DM in their overcrowded inbox. Instead, consider how you or your business can help them add value to a story they are writing. My strategy was always reaching out, mentioning a piece of theirs that I have read and liked, and simply stating that if they ever need any help for a relevant story, I would be very happy to contribute a quote or anything they need. Most of the time, they would be working on a story they could use an extra quote or case study for. That is how I ended up being featured on Business Insider multiple times, the Wall Street Journal, Fast Company and more.

The very first feature came around six weeks after I launched my business, and it was on Business Insider, in an article about how Gen Zers are starting their own marketing consultancies – so extremely relevant. This one article brought multiple clients my way, and because it ranked high on SEO, it kept working in my favour for months. All of that from a single Twitter/X DM that took five minutes. An important point to note here is that it is important that the account you message someone from seems credible. You can always email, but it is harder to stand out that way. I used Twitter/X because I already had a few thousand followers and seemed like I wasn't a spammer who was trying to sell something. If you do this on whichever platform you think you appear more credible, you will have a higher chance of people responding and taking you seriously. You have absolutely nothing to lose. So much could come from simply reaching out to people and building relationships, so if you are not doing that already, it is time to start!

Curating your content

Content creation takes time. Most of us do not generate great new ideas and original thoughts every day, but thankfully, there is a way around that. Becoming a good curator of content can be one of the skills that make you invaluable. If you read a lot, have a collection of interesting articles, tools and resources, or just spend a lot of time consuming other people's content, you could be an excellent content curator. Curated content can be a part of your content strategy. Essentially, it means sharing content or ideas you have stumbled upon and found interesting. As you build credibility over time, your audience will value what you share because it saves them the time and effort of searching through content themselves. Good curation allows you to build an audience that trusts your taste. If you are someone that people come to for recommendations often, that is a good sign that you might have an eye for finding interesting things. This is a strength you can use to build your personal brand, on any social media platform, or even through a newsletter. Countless newsletters focus on concepts like 'five interesting links per week', and have an audience simply because they seem to always be finding valuable things to share. It is an effective way to build a community, establish your presence in an industry and connect with like-minded people. Some examples of such content formats that could work across most social media platforms are posts like 'the best things I read this week' (e.g. articles or essays), 'five websites/tools to achieve [...]', 'creators to follow if you are interested in [...]', 'my favourite podcast episodes related to [...]' and so on.

You would be surprised at how interested people can be in what you are reading, listening to and exploring. It is a very easy way to keep yourself active when it comes to creating content, just by sharing what you are already doing. Develop a habit of saving the interesting things you stumble upon. I have a running list of links and ideas that sparked my interest (I use Notion to organize them and tag them by topic) so that any time I am stuck on what content I could create, I can always simply share something useful. As long as you are sharing things that you find useful or insightful, there will be people out there that find them useful and insightful too. If you are interested in the idea of becoming more intentional about your content consumption and collecting valuable things, Tiago Forte's *Building a Second Brain* methodology could be for you: it revolves around taking digital notes of every idea that sparks your interest, every insight you stumble upon that you want to store for future reference and thus developing an organizational system that ensures you will never forget the countless interesting things you stumble upon every day. According to Forte, 'a study cited by the *Times* estimates that we consume the equivalent of 174 full newspapers' worth of content each and every day, five times higher than in 1986.' Naturally, that is an incredible amount of information for our brains to process, let alone filter and remember. Creating a personal knowledge management system will not only transform your relationship to the information you consume, it will also make you a great curator of content. If another impactful habit comes out of building your personal brand, this could be it.

Personal branding pitfalls

While there is no one-size-fits-all for personal branding strategies, there are a few things that I would recommend avoiding, and common mistakes people make. The first one is over-promotion. There are many cases where people tend to over-promote: when they offer services, when they have their own business, a project or a newsletter, for example. It is tempting to keep reminding your audience what you do through your content, so you can redirect them somewhere beyond your content. But over-promotion gets tiring for your audience, and it can make you seem ungenuine or inauthentic. You should definitely include promotion in your content from time to time if you have something to offer or a project you are trying to grow, but the key is keeping it balanced. It should not be your primary content pillar.

Another common pitfall is inconsistency. You can have a great content strategy but you will fail to see results if you post once per month. Of course, the more consistent you are, the more likely you are to build an audience, but that is not to say that you have to post every day. You are the only one who knows what schedule is realistic and sustainable for you, but even posting on LinkedIn two or three times per week can work wonders over time. The same goes for TikTok, where you often hear that you will only build an audience if you post at least once a day. While that helps, quality matters more – just deliver it consistently in your own schedule. On Twitter/X it is easier to remain consistent, because the barrier to content creation is the lowest: you simply type out a quick thought, update or idea in a minute and share it. No matter what schedule and platform you choose, consistency is what will propel you forward if you give it some time.

Finally, the biggest one: assuming that building a personal brand is all you need to do to find recognition and success. Your personal brand cannot help you if you do not take the time to develop the skills that will make people want to work with you. It will lead those people to you, but it is up to you to turn yourself into someone that people want to collaborate with. Cameron Dower, a Gen Z entrepreneur who has used his personal brand to build a marketing agency and land clients, emphasizes the fact that a personal brand is an amplification tool: 'It amplifies what you can bring to the table. If you have nothing to bring to the table, what's the point? Build skills first, then build credibility through a personal brand.' Your personal brand will be successful if you have the skills to back it. So, if you decide to invest time and effort into growing your personal brand, make sure more of your energy is spent cultivating the skills that will help you stand out.

Authenticity vs. professionalism

It can be difficult to know how to balance your authentic, unfiltered self with your more professional side. This balance is vital, as you do not want to be unfiltered to the point where all your posts cause controversy (this is one way to get engagement but truly not a great one), but as I have stressed in this chapter, being authentic is the only way for you to stand out. If everyone was to create the same monotonous, professional content, then social media would lose all its value. Having a unique voice is an advantage – use it. Authenticity can be embedded both in your voice and in the types of content you post. Professionalism is more about knowing where to draw the line between oversharing and being vulnerable for the sake of allowing your audience to get to know you better.

To be vulnerable and authentic means to be comfortable with being genuine. Sharing your mistakes, honest experiences and learnings reminds people that you are more than just a face on a screen. It makes you relatable, and thus more interesting. Being genuine is at the core of building a community online. If community is one of your goals, with an audience that will remain engaged and interested in your content and your work, then you have to let go of the urge to be perfect. Perfectionism is the enemy of consistency and authenticity, do not let it get the best of you and hold you back. If you self-identify as a perfectionist more than you identify as someone who gets things done, it is so important to turn that around. Perfectionism will not get you far, but learning to get things done will.

A key trait to develop here is confidence. Without it, being yourself and authentically creating content and showing up online is almost impossible. Many people are held back by the insecurity and fear of what others will think of their content, or of the very fact that they are posting online to begin with. But if other people judge you for showing up and being proactive, that is their problem to deal with, not yours. Those who take the initiative and are not afraid to take up space eventually stand out, it is as simple as that. Do not let yourself shrink your potential and your voice because of a fear of judgement. Any judgement that might arise will be inconsequential compared to all the opportunities and the growth that you will be exposing yourself to. The path to growth is not always comfortable, but it is worth it. Jaiya Gill, a Gen Z entrepreneur, marketer and social media strategist, quit her corporate finance career when she realized that her job, lacking autonomy or meaning, was hindering her from figuring out what she really wanted to do. She took the time to explore her options and started creating content on social media while looking into the tech startup world. She credits the personal brand she built as the catalyst that launched her corporate to startup career change. Once she found the confidence to start posting online, she also found that she felt a lot more assured about her career in general, like she could pursue anything she wanted to do. In that way, putting yourself out there can help you think bigger, and internalize the ability to set bigger goals. The personal brand Jaiya developed helped her stand out among the competitive tech startup scene, allowing her to meet people and access opportunities by showing up authentically: 'Basically, my people found me. All I had to do was be myself and find my niche.'

It is completely normal and very common to struggle with building confidence and overcoming self-doubt. Doing anything that requires putting yourself out there for the first time naturally causes fear and overthinking. Here are some practical steps you can take to overcome this:

- Start small. You do not have to post the most thought-provoking and viral piece of content to start building your personal brand. The best thing you can do is just start *somewhere*, so get yourself used to creating and posting content little by little.
- Talk to people you know that you think have a great personal brand. Ask them how they started posting more online, what they have learned along the way and what they would do differently if they were just starting out. By talking to people you will also come to realize that everyone feels this way at the beginning.
- Engage with others. Even if you do not feel ready to start creating your own content, getting used to engaging with others' content is one step closer to voicing your thoughts in public. It will get you used to the fact that people are reading what you have to say.
- Focus on value over approval. Instead of focusing on whether a post got enough likes or comments, focus on producing content that you *know* is valuable and

helpful to a certain audience. Knowing that your content is useful to someone will help you detach from social media metrics, and keep going.

Twitter/X

Let's get into the practical steps you can take on each platform, starting with Twitter/X. Begin with a profile makeover, because aesthetics matter more than you think. It is absolutely subjective, of course, but here are some things that I would advise: choose a good profile picture that will be recognizable when someone sees it on their feed. It definitely doesn't have to be overly professional, because Twitter/X is more of a casual platform compared to others like LinkedIn. So, no corporate headshots are needed. Your profile should also have a header that either adds to its aesthetic appeal or communicates something extra about you. An aesthetically pleasing header can bind your profile together and make it look more cohesive and less chaotic when someone stumbles upon it, making them more likely to follow. On the other hand, a header that communicates something about you could include a quote that represents you or something similar, because there are only so many things you can say in your bio to present yourself. On to the dreaded bio: presenting who you are and what you do in a couple of sentences or keywords, no pressure. Keep it simple and concise. Decide what points you want to get across and focus on conveying them. Everything else, people will discover through your tweets as they get to know you.

An important point here is that if you do many different things, that is also fine. Social media creates the unnecessary stress of unrealistically having to fit ourselves in a box, in order for our personal brand to be more digestible. Some people are lucky enough to have one single niche that they want to stick to, and that they are extremely passionate about. That definitely makes personal branding easier, but it is not a requirement. Being multi-disciplinary or difficult to categorize can be an advantage, helping you stand out. By refusing to be categorized, you're also establishing yourself as someone who is authentic and unique. So, while having a field around which your personal brand will revolve is what will help you attract opportunities, you don't have to limit yourself to talking only about that. Sometimes your different interests can give you learnings that are transferrable to other areas of your life and work, making your perspective more unique. As a tangible example, my own bio references my founder/CEO title at my company (to reach the entrepreneurship community), the fact that I'm a writer (because I want to connect with more writers) and my hobby as a travel photographer, which is also something I am very passionate about. All this does is build a more well-rounded image of who I am and consequently helps me connect with more like-minded people, which enriches my life. When writing your bio, keep in mind that it should give people an idea of what they should expect your tweets to be about if they follow you. Some people's bios very clearly state 'Tweets about remote work, startups and investing', for example. That facilitates the decisive moment where someone stumbles upon your profile and makes a choice to either follow you or scroll past.

When it comes to Twitter/X, you might need to unlearn what you think you know about the platform. The most essential point to keep in mind, and something I always advise brands and people alike, is that you don't have to overthink it or take a formal approach. Authentic, original thoughts that are worded casually and conversationally are the way to go. You can share a quote you like, an idea from a book, a quick life update, a funny thought, an interesting article. They have a short lifespan on people's feeds, so they disappear quickly, lowering the stakes. The ideal mix of content is a balance between thought-out, purposely interesting tweets and more casual and conversational updates that will help you build trust with your followers and be more human. In terms of quantity of posting, tweets are again more like Instagram Stories: it is fine if you post two or three a day, whereas on LinkedIn that could appear as spammy. Also, you do not need to use hashtags in your tweets, unless they are for a specific event, live tweeting occasion or a branded campaign. Twitter/X's search finds in-text keywords anyway, so all generic hashtags like #marketing will do is make your posts appear more crowded and spammy. You also do not have to limit yourself only to posts that fit within the platform's character limit. A common practice on the platform is posting threads (successive tweets that are connected) to share long-form content. The first tweet can be about hooking the reader with an intriguing premise and setting the topic, so that they want to read the tweets that follow underneath it. High-quality threads that share a lot of value have good virality potential and are a great way to present more of your insights, thoughts and ideas to your audience, so they can get to know you better. They are also great for storytelling, or for content formats like 'Ten things I learned from [this experience]'.

Ari Dutilh is an 18-year-old founder who created two online communities with thousands of members all around the world, and is also building a biotech startup while finishing high school. He recognizes building a small follower base on Twitter/X as what led to every single major opportunity he has been able to access, including securing the grant funding for his biotech startup, UltraRice. In his experience so far, building a Twitter/X presence has had 'an astronomical impact' on his career. For those looking to access opportunities and network in the entrepreneurship and tech scene, Twitter/X can indeed be second to none. The organic community that has been created around these topics is very active, and offers a level of access that, in this niche, has not been replicated on any other social media platform. In many cases, if an entrepreneur or mentor you want to connect with is active on Twitter/X, they will likely be more open to receiving direct messages there than on LinkedIn, where their inbox is full of daily spam. Those with 'Founder' or 'CEO' in their title are so often the subjects of automated sales messages on LinkedIn, used as one of the biggest growth channels for outbound sales, to the extent where they can easily miss even the interesting messages coming through. Twitter/X is different. Not devoid of spam itself, it is seen as more of a community-driven platform where the intent of networking is often more genuine and less focused on just selling to someone.

It is worth noting that since July 2023, when Twitter rebranded to X under Elon Musk's new leadership, the platform has become more unpredictable. Features have been coming and going, making it more unreliable for creators. Through its new paid subscription, the platform now rewards those who pay a yearly or monthly fee with increased prioritization, fewer ads and other features. Is the premium subscription worth it for content creators? It depends. Since premium users' post replies are prioritized in the algorithm, it can give your content wider reach. It also offers the ability to edit posts and post longer content. If you are very serious about your Twitter/X presence, this can potentially be helpful, but it is not at all necessary to ensure your account's growth and reach.

LinkedIn

The core of building a personal brand remains the same across platforms, but there are important differentiators. Moving on to LinkedIn: it is of course more professional, less casual and more formal than Twitter. Across most industries, it is useful for you to be active on LinkedIn, simply because it makes it so easy to find the right people to connect with. Whether you want to work with a brand, at a brand or get featured in the press, you can find the relevant decision-makers and engage with them quite easily. Most young professionals are only active on LinkedIn to send the occasional connection request, find open roles or see what others are up to. Making a habit of posting on the platform will immediately differentiate you, because it definitely takes more effort, and shows that you are committed to taking the initiative and being active in your field.

So, what should you post? It highly depends on your industry. In the marketing industry, for example, accounts with very few followers have gone viral just for spotting an interesting brand campaign and talking about it before anyone else does. Deconstructing trends, spotting unique marketing initiatives and sharing case studies are some other types of posts that work well. If your post gets early traction, the algorithm pushes it to many new people's feeds, so your reach can quickly spread far beyond your network. Just like on any platform, see what types of posts work best for your specific industry and identify where you could share some value; is there a gap you can fill? Treat your content strategy like it's a brand: identifying broad pillars that your content should fit into, such as educational content, and managing to offer something engaging within that. Educational content is a timeless pillar because it can work so well. Everyone loves learning something interesting. So, if you can offer that, people are likely to follow you for more.

More casual updates can also work well on LinkedIn if executed in the right way. If you just started a new job, you could post a behind-the-scenes of your first day, or share something you learned; it does not have to be ground-breaking. Another way you can stand out on LinkedIn is by developing a visual style and accompanying your posts with recognizable graphics. If you are skilled at creating text-based content, you could also consider starting a regular content series on the platform, providing your audience with consistent value after figuring out what they are interested in. If a specific post format or topic seems to work well, think about how you can replicate that consistently while keeping it engaging.

Meagan Loyst, founder of Gen Z VCs, an online community with over 25,000 members, uses LinkedIn to attract all kinds of opportunities and grow her personal brand. For new creators looking to break into the platform, she advises:

> The most important thing is creating content that adds value, is net-new and has some viral component. My viral 26-page metaverse manifesto has been read by millions of people and still opens doors to this day. For the creators just starting out, first think through your niche – what perspective is underappreciated on LinkedIn where you could add a new voice? And then start posting consistently 3x a week!

But of course, that is not enough to stand out among the noise. Meagan notices that the best posts stem from personal experience, where someone can help others develop the same skills or learn something from them, bringing us back to the idea of educational content. 'Really think deep about who comes to you for advice, for what, and why … that's usually a good place to start. Unpack that and lean into it.' That is a great approach for figuring out your uniqueness: What are you people's go-to person for? Is there any pattern that arises in the things your friends come to you for? You might be very skilled at time management or problem-solving. Take some time to think about all of this and it will help you create content providing the type of unique value only you can offer.

TikTok

If you are looking for something more casual and fun, then TikTok could be the right platform for your personal brand. It works better in some industries than others, and naturally more visual industries are easier to create content for. Designers, marketers and artists of any kind go viral daily on the platform for sharing their work and providing inspiration. But even if your industry is completely different, TikTok provides an opportunity to creatively come up with innovative content that will stand out. Niche channels can have great success; all you have to do is be authentic and experiment. Learning from what works for other people is important, but even more important is remaining true to yourself in your content, so that it is scalable, real and enjoyable for you to create. TikTok is a natural platform for storytelling and content that allows your audience to get to know you better. Where Twitter is more conversational and LinkedIn more formal, TikTok provides a platform for you to go one step deeper and embrace your most human side.

There are two key types of value you can provide through your content: educational or entertaining. The ideal is if you can combine the two and take an 'edutainment' approach. This will make your content more memorable and will likely increase how much people enjoy consuming and sharing it with others. Another popular type of content that performs well on TikTok is aspirational or inspirational lifestyle content. What do you enjoy creating the most? There is space for everyone; as long as you create content you enjoy and remain consistent, you will find your people and build your personal brand. For those in more creative careers, TikTok can definitely lead to faster growth than other platforms and bring more opportunities your way. Think about who you want to reach through your personal brand. If your target audience is corporate recruiters, your efforts are probably better spent on LinkedIn than on TikTok. But if you are in the fashion industry and are looking to find people to collaborate with, like designers or photographers, TikTok is the way to go.

But you are an ambitious person, and you have many different goals... So how do you balance them all? Your personal brand is not a monolith. You can use different platforms for different purposes, spreading your efforts however you can. Personally, I am focused on Twitter/X for general industry connections and finding fellow Gen Z entrepreneurs, and on LinkedIn for attracting speaking engagements or press. All other platforms I use have a more personal rather than professional focus: TikTok for my hobbies, Instagram for friends. It is a mix I have found to work well for me, but it might be different for you. Experimenting pays off.

Instagram

If you are starting to build your personal brand from scratch, Instagram can be helpful but especially so for some specific industries. If your goal is to become a content creator with the aim of being an influencer, Instagram can be as useful as TikTok. The downside is that its algorithm makes it harder, in most cases, to get wide reach when you are starting from zero (contrary to TikTok, which can make it very easy for that to happen if you understand your audience well and post consistently). Of course there are exceptions. If you post videos (Reels), they have a much higher chance at going viral and bringing you a large amount of new followers, if you get lucky. Some people have better luck posting consistent Instagram Reels rather than TikToks. It is a mix of luck and algorithm preferences that you just need to experiment with and see how it goes. As of late 2023, video content is currently at the forefront on Instagram, so if you can generate video content as part of your personal brand you have a higher chance of growing your account. However, these algorithmic preferences change all the time, and we have no way of knowing whether in a few months or years the platform will once again push photo posts more actively. Understanding where you should focus your efforts requires also spending some time staying informed with social media updates and platform changes, so you can always be adapting your strategy according to available data.

Contrary to Twitter/X, Instagram is a platform that most young people would expect almost anyone to be on. It is becoming what Facebook used to be. It is your choice whether you will keep your Instagram more personal and private, or open it up to being a part of your personal brand, where you also share content related to your work and your chosen area of interest.

There are ways to increase your discoverability on Instagram if you choose to focus on this platform. Adding a couple of relevant keywords to your display name, for example, can make your account show up when people search about your niche. So if you are posting professional content in some way, for example in the social media marketing niche, your display name can be '[Your Name] – Social Media Marketer' to increase the chances that people looking for marketers will find you. My biggest trick to increase reach on Instagram is actually having a good hashtag strategy. Many people believe hashtags do not really work any more, but they have worked wonders for many brand accounts I have managed as part of my marketing agency, often increasing their posts' organic reach by 50 per cent or more. You just need to do some good keyword research, and ideally use all 30 hashtags that Instagram allows you to use per post.

Instagram also has another advantage worth noting: its features are inherently more community-driven than TikTok's. Instagram Story features, like polls and questions, allow creators to engage with their audience in a much more active way. Users are also a lot more used to watching and interacting with Instagram Stories, than they are to watching TikTok Stories. Community should be one of your core goals if you are creating content on social media to build your personal brand. It means that more than having people simply follow you, you attract those who will love interacting with your content, giving you feedback, and supporting you. So Instagram's community-focused features are a great way to boost that engagement and interact with your audience more intentionally.

Personal websites and blogs

At some point the time will come when you will ask yourself whether you should also have a personal website. At the very start of your personal branding journey, I would not say it is necessary. But later on, it is definitely a welcome addition, with two main benefits: firstly, it makes you extra easy to find. When someone looks you up, which they will, having a personal website allows you to convey all the important information about yourself and direct people to the right places. Almost every thought leader you follow on social media probably has some type of personal website. It is a way to have more ownership over how you present yourself online, and create your own corner of the internet that remains intact no matter how social media platforms change. It is a more holistic way to combine your work, interests and skills, while showcasing your individuality. Especially if you are a creative, a personal website allows you to present your style and stand out.

In many cases, personal websites go hand in hand with writing online. Social media content is great, but more tailored, long-form content like blogs has proven again and again to be extremely beneficial in many ways. In the ways that social media content brings the right people to you, writing online shows people more of who you are. Having a blog, whether on your own website or on a plat-form like Substack, creates a whole new growth channel that you can utilize as you grow and shape your career. A newsletter is a great way to deliver consistent value to an audience in a more flexible format than social media. A newsletter is also more scalable: it can become a proper business or side gig. Three popular platforms to host a blog or newsletter are Substack, Medium and Beehiiv. Choosing one depends on your priorities and the features that matter most to you. Medium posts tend to rank higher than the rest on SEO, so if you write about topics that people are likely to be searching for a lot, it could facilitate discoverability. Substack has a great community and a social interface, allowing you to join an ecosystem of writers and engage with your favourite creators easily. Beehiiv is popular for its monetization features, and better for those looking to grow a newsletter as a business. So depending on your interests, starting a blog or newsletter should be something to consider; remember, everyone has something to share, and that includes you.

In the book *Show Your Work*, Austin Kleon states that 'Carving out a space for yourself online, somewhere where you can express yourself and share your work, is still one of the best possible investments you can make with your time.' He advocates for creating a personal website that is uniquely yours:

> Social networks are great, but they come and go. (Remember Myspace? Friendster? GeoCities?) If you're really interested in sharing your work and expressing yourself, nothing beats owning your own space online, a space that you can control, a place that no one can take away from you, a world headquarters where people can always find you.

Action plan

It is time to put everything into action. Here is your checklist to begin your personal branding journey:

1 Identify the things that make you unique. Your specific knowledge, the things your friends come to you for

advice on and, of course, the things you are most interested in talking about. Make sure you know what topics you want to become associated with.

2 Look into the current online space in your niche. Identify the top thought leaders and key voices. Do a deep dive and discover which social media platforms are getting the most traction in your niche, where there may be a gap you could fill with your content, and what types of content are performing best. This is how you will create a strong personal branding strategy.

3 Decide on how often you will post and where. Make a commitment to yourself and stick to it. Set a plan to post three times per week on LinkedIn, for example, and add it to your schedule. Remember: you have to start somewhere, do not wait for the perfect moment. Becoming a doer is what will set you apart. Everyone wants to start something at some point, but very few people actually do. Getting things done is one of the most important skills you will ever cultivate, and sticking to a commitment related to your personal brand is a great way to start.

4 Revamp your relevant social media profiles to make sure they are up to date. Make them keyword-optimized in a way that makes it easy for the right people to find you.

5 Start posting. Experiment with different types of content, then look at your social media analytics at the end of each month and learn from them. Adapt your strategy as needed. It is a continuous learning process, so be very open to change and to learning from your own experience.

6 Start engaging. Identify the people you want to connect with, as clients, mentors, business partners. Get yourself used to 'shooting your shot' – introduce yourself and offer value and support where you can. Remember that people care about what *you* can bring to the table and contribute, so keep that in mind when reaching out. Yes, a lot of people will also connect with you and jump on a call because they love to help out, but it is rare, and everyone's time is precious. Build genuine relationships and become a supportive and welcoming voice for your network. Become a connector, and help people out by directing relevant opportunities their way. If you give, you will receive: that is at the core of engaging.

In this digital landscape, personal branding is not just a nice-to-have, but a critical component to facilitate your professional success. To create a career on your own terms, you have to put yourself out there, curate your online presence and learn to create a network that will push you forward. By making a point of intentionally being authentic and consistent with your content, the aim is to go beyond simply being noticed, to being remembered for the right reasons. Become findable, take the risk of standing out, and it can have a very real impact on your success in creating a fulfilling professional path.

Notes

1   Jacobs, D L (2013) How an online reputation can hurt your job hunt, Forbes. www.forbes.com/sites/deborahljacobs/2013/05/17/how-an-online-reputation-can-hurt-your-job-hunt/#:~:text=In%20fact%2C%20 90%25%20of%20executive,found%20out%20about%20them%20 online (archived at https://perma.cc/U4RS-K43A)
2   Vaden, R Why you need a personal brand, https://roryvaden.com/blog/ personal-branding/why-you-need-a-personal-brand/ (archived at https:// perma.cc/7SH9-BVDN)
3   Weinswig, D (2016) Influencers are the new brands, www.forbes.com/ sites/deborahweinswig/2016/10/05/influencers-are-the-new-brands/?sh=2aac89db7919 (archived at https://perma.cc/2D3H-REPG)

CHAPTER SIX

Chasing trends and opportunities

Figuring out exactly what type of independent work to pursue is not always simple: you know your own skills, you know your preferences and the problems you would enjoy solving through your work, but how do you identify whether an opportunity is worth pursuing? Trends come and go, and, as we've seen, the world of trends and opportunities moves fast. Startups have gotten very lucky by jumping on the right trend at the right time, while others have failed as a result of going all in on an opportunity that ended up being just a short-lived fad. This goes for industry trends, marketing trends and everything in between; trends have a lifecycle, and knowing how to navigate and understand it can provide you with a big advantage in business and entrepreneurship. This chapter is most useful for those who are interested in entrepreneurship or marketing, where being able to spot and analyse trends and opportunities can be very rewarding and impactful.

If you're reading this book, chances are you are considering working for yourself in some way – even if you don't aim to become an entrepreneur, you may want to work at a startup that offers flexible ways of working and allows you to design your life around that. Even in that case, spotting trends and opportunities is essential – you don't want to dedicate your time and career to something that may seem like a promising opportunity but eventually ends up going under, which is so common with startups. Nine out of ten startups fail, with the primary reason being that they were building something the market did not need.[1] They believed they had an idea that people wanted, only to end up discovering that what seemed like an opportunity was in fact destined to fail.

Identifying business opportunities

So, how do you go about evaluating opportunities and taking advantage of them early on? I looked into in-depth research on trend lifecycles and interviewed experts with a track record of identifying trends and opportunities early, to draw out the best strategies that you can use as well – consider this chapter as a (much cheaper) mini-MBA. Harvard Business School Professor Clayton Christensen suggests a structured approach to identifying opportunities.[2] First, he points out that there are three types of business opportunities to search for: the Jobs to Be Done, the low-end market opportunities and the new market opportunities.

The Jobs to Be Done theory has been widely renowned for suggesting that people don't *buy* a product, they *hire* it to do a job. In that way, it considers that people don't buy coffee – they hire it to keep them awake and give them energy. To understand and apply the Jobs to Be Done theory, you must first identify jobs that consumers want to get done. 'Jobs' here is a wide term to suggest all the things people need done in their everyday lives. That includes any type of problem they want to solve. Your task here is to identify those 'jobs' when you see them, and ask yourself if a product/service already exists to solve them, and if it does, whether there is room for it to be significantly improved. So when evaluating a business opportunity, you can run it through this test of seeing whether it meets a need for a job that people need done. To figure out what people actually *need* done and ensure that you are not generalizing, there are specific strategies you can follow, which we will discuss later on in this chapter. Then, Christensen's theories go into what he calls disruptive innovation; understanding them can help you make more informed decisions if or when you consider building a business.

Low-end market disruption is when you identify a market where a large competitor already holds a significant share, and you see space for a new business to enter the low end of that market, going for a very low-profit business model. The established competitor rarely reacts, because they don't perceive the low-end entry as a threat. Starting off with simple and cheap solutions, you target the consumers at the low end of that market that only have basic needs that can be easily met, and then you advance your business as you go on, and move higher through the market. This type of business also fuels innovation – it usually targets markets where the established businesses have grown stagnant, and offers a fresh perspective that slowly shakes things up from the ground up. An example of that is Southwest Airlines: when they entered the industry, the established airlines were focusing on high-end airline services, offering high-class seating, upgrade options, in-flight meals and so on. Southwest saw an opportunity in the low end of the market, to serve the customers that were budget-conscious and were looking for simple and affordable air travel solutions. They entered the market by offering much lower pricing than competitors, reducing costs by using only one specific type of aircraft, and so managing to attract an underserved market segment.

The other type of disruptive innovation is new-market disruption. This is when you identify a segment of consumers that is overserved by the current products or services trying to meet their needs: for example, the established companies trying to solve one of their problems are offering too many unnecessary features for a higher price, and this consumer segment just wants something simpler, cheaper and that is just 'good enough'. Can you think of a time where you felt like that? Starting from your own experiences can be insightful. Pay attention to the times when you or someone around you thought 'I want a product like this, but it's too expensive... I wish there was something simpler that I could get for a lower price. I don't need all this.' This is where new-market disruption can happen. Businesses identifying such opportunities are creating new segments in an existing market, to serve consumers differently and more accurately. To create and meet the needs of that new segment, aim to create something that's cheaper than the current options, and of 'good enough' quality. Because you're going for the low end of the market that needs simpler solutions for less money, perfecting the product doesn't matter as much as making it simply *good enough* to capture that audience with unmet needs. So, think of whether you have ever noticed a market that seems to be overserving people with no simpler solution. It's easy and common for established companies to start adding more and more features and raising their pricing as they grow, forgetting about the simplicity and accessibility that many consumers still need. An example of new market disruption is when simple digital cameras entered the market. Up until that point, the photography market was dominated by high-end digital cameras or traditional film cameras, both not really suitable for the type of consumer that just wanted something simple, affordable and just 'good enough' to get the job done. The existing options were too complex to operate and often too expensive for the average consumer who just wanted a way to quickly shoot and view digital photos without needing any more features. The introduction of affordable, easy-to-use digital cameras targeted that type of consumer and met that previously unsolved need.

Understanding these three types of market opportunities can be a useful starting point when evaluating business ideas. But how do you come up with ideas in the first place? When it comes to creating new products or services, sometimes the best ideas just come to you as a result of the conversations you have, the people you meet or the media you read and consume. But there are ways to trigger that process and think of new ideas in a more intentional way. The first way to spot an opportunity is, naturally, to start with yourself. What are your pain points or problems that do not seem to have the right solution? In my case, I started The Z Link after noticing time and time again that companies I worked for were asking me the same questions: how do we connect with Gen Z? As a Gen Zer myself, one of my pain points was that I was tired of being bombarded by ads on social media that seemed so out of tune with what I would actually want to see, and what would bring some value to my life. Most of them simply seemed... disconnected. I thought, surely we can do a lot better than that – if I have to see hundreds of posts on my feed every day by brands trying to target me, they might as well learn to understand me and my generation, and what we *actually* want. So, The Z Link was born: with a mix of social media marketing and market research, I embarked on the journey of trying to help the world better understand generational behaviours, and make marketing more human and more of a two-way conversation. Today, our research has ended up being used even to help employers work with Gen Z and shape the future of work with our generation in mind. As it turned out, the small opportunity I spotted through my own pain points had even more demand than I originally expected. Through this example, you can see that a successful and promising opportunity can arise from just an observation, by paying attention to things in your own life.

The other way to discover new ideas more intentionally is to question the process.[3] Take an area or problem you are interested in, and see how the current processes that exist to solve it can be improved. Can it be made faster, more efficient, simpler? Can the current processes and businesses that exist be made cheaper but retain the quality expected by consumers? Can they be made more accessible or more sustainable? You can find an area of improvement and work on that. To better understand that, there are many good examples we can point to. One is food delivery apps. Food delivery existed before them, but it was handled by the restaurants directly. This was not very efficient, being an often slow and limited process. Apps like Uber Eats, Deliveroo and DoorDash came in and revolutionized that process, making food delivery more reliable (consumers now know exactly how long their delivery will take, they can track it live and solve issues easily through the platform), and more efficient (being able to access a database of available restaurants and browse their menus in one place is of course a lot more convenient). Another example is telehealth platforms like Teladoc in the US. They questioned the process of seeing a doctor, its convenience and accessibility. It was inaccessible and difficult for people in remote areas, and usually far more time-consuming than most people could manage. It also didn't always justify going in-person, for consultations that could successfully be done remotely. Telehealth platforms addressed that part of the process and improved it by offering an easy way for people to consult doctors remotely, via phone or video, making the healthcare process faster and more inclusive. Entrepreneurship can often sound like an intimidating process that requires ground-breaking ideas and innovation, but that's not the case. You can be doing something new and needed without reinventing the wheel. It's often as simple as recognizing a problem shared by a community, or a process that can be improved in some areas, and working to address that.

In many cases, if you have a problem, that means a lot of other people probably do too. So, how do you make sure that's the case?

Market research

Your best friend when evaluating and identifying business opportunities should be market research. A simple Google search won't cut it – you will have to go further than that to access the type of data that is most valuable. When conducting market research, you basically want to use all the methods that will give you the type of information that is most insightful, so that you can uncover trends that are less obvious. I spoke to Michael Daigler, an entrepreneur and software engineer working in the areas of tech and AI. His approach is a unique one that I had not heard before: he identifies trends and opportunities by taking a community-first approach. 'The way I discern what's a good opportunity and what's not, is by looking at whether it has a strong community around it.'

Conducting market research through online communities can be very informative: you can tap into the common problems, patterns and conversations that arise in a community that is engaged around one shared topic.

Through platforms like Reddit, you can find the spaces on the internet where people most actively engage around an interest. Of course, it helps if you look into communities around topics that you have a personal interest in yourself, as well. This will allow you to navigate and understand them and their pain points better, and ultimately, you do not want to be building a product or service around an area that seems profitable but that you have no further interest in at all. Being driven by a real curiosity about the problem and the domain is a big advantage; entrepreneurship is no easy journey, and sustaining passion, personal interest and genuine curiosity will help you succeed. Being driven by profitability alone is a recipe for failure.

So, based on your interests, consider what active communities exist on the internet on platforms such as Reddit that you can explore and research. What you will find is that you sometimes start with a wide topic in mind, and end up finding smaller and smaller sub-communities within it that you can tap into. All it takes is finding a pain point that is common and prevalent within one of these communities, and you have potential for a viable and useful idea. However, there is a fine balance – Daigler acknowledged that there is such a thing as too niche, and that can lead a lot of opportunities that originally seemed promising to eventually fail. Having worked actively in the crypto and NFT space, Daigler saw first-hand how largely a trend can get overestimated due to one community's excitement and investment. A while ago, investors were pouring money into startups building in the space of NFTs, in what seemed to be the next big market opportunity. Starting from quite a niche community of crypto enthusiasts, the conversation quickly became mainstream and reached everyone else too. Before you knew it, everyone was looking into NFTs and wondering if they should be investing in these digital assets. But as we saw in the months that followed, the hype died down, and the amount of people that actually profited off the opportunity was much smaller than what the mainstream conversation made it out to seem like. One example is the Bored Ape Yacht Club (BAYC), which was valued at more than $400,000 at the time of its peak in April 2022. By July 2023, it had plummeted to around $52,000, a nearly 88 per cent drop in value from its peak. Daigler also points out that there was too big a learning curve for the NFT trend to become as global an opportunity as many expected it to be. There was a general lack of clarity around the topic, where a very small percentage of people involved in the industry fully understood how it worked. Rather than clarity and simplicity, what prevailed was confusion and noise. Now, when he evaluates trends and potential opportunities, Daigler sticks to an approach of 'the simpler it is, the better'. It does not have to be complicated to succeed, quite the opposite: the sweet spot of promising trends/opportunities tends to be where a problem a community is facing is solved, in a simple and straightforward way. If you have spotted an opportunity that seems to fit within that description, you may have something good in your hands.

When conducting market research, it is also essential to go more in-depth than we are used to going due to our relationship with social media. A lot of us tend to assume, even subconsciously, that we can get a lot of the valuable information we need on social media. While that is true, we overestimate the quality of that information, and I am not even referring to the amount of misleading low-quality information that is present everywhere. I am referring to the depth in which that information goes on those platforms. During our conversation, Daigler mentioned how important it is to broaden your information sources and focus on all the deep knowledge that is out there in other formats, which because of social media, we tend to overlook. Today, it is common for our generation to research a topic on TikTok or Twitter/X, to follow creators that post about a certain niche and believe that we are getting sufficient information on it. But that is only allowing us to access one tenth of the information that is available on a topic we choose. Instead, Daigler's approach is finding books that dive into a certain topic because they naturally examine it a lot more in-depth than we see on social media, and because the author has usually done more research and made a very active effort to put all the most useful insights together in a book that can be as helpful and informative as possible. As niche as the area you are researching may be, there is probably a book on it, and it will likely give you a much deeper understanding of its ins and outs than TikTok will. It will give you access to a depth of knowledge and insight that is rarely brought to the surface through social media or quick Google research. To add to Daigler's approach, my suggestion would be using books to construct your research foundation, and social media to conduct social listening and understand the public sentiment on something. TikTok, Twitter/X and Reddit can all provide insight into where the public conversations around a certain topic are, and that is definitely useful. You can evaluate whether the prevailing sentiment on a topic is positive or negative, for example, and access the most engaged conversations taking place around it.

Besides books and social media, there are some other excellent sources you can use to conduct market research and to stay up to date with emerging trends, making sure that they will appear on your radar. Everyone I interviewed for this chapter has their own favourite resources that they use, and their own process for staying informed with new trends and opportunities. It is never a passive process: even when you are not actively researching something through books, social media or online communities, it is a combination of the resources you surround yourself with, the newsletters you subscribe to and the intentional ways in which you consume content online. Here are some resources that were mentioned by one or more trends experts, so you can stay up to date with emerging areas and spot patterns:

- Trends: Mentioned in a previous chapter as well, this community and newsletter by The Hustle offers a very straightforward way to get informed about new trends, see the data that proves they are on the rise and read about businesses that are profiting off similar opportunities. I love the no-noise and high-value nature of their newsletter, which provides a standardized way to see interesting data and find out about niche areas on the rise that could have easily slipped through your radar otherwise.

- GummySearch.com: GummySearch is an audience research tool that allows you to search for pain points, solutions to be built, content ideas, sales leads and more, based on thousands of subreddit communities on Reddit. For any type of niche you choose, it shows you common patterns that emerge in related subreddits, like usual problems that users post about, solutions they are asking for and more. It is designed to help users find startup ideas and validate product demand, so it is perfect for this type of trend analysis.
- Explodingtopics.com: This website presents rapidly growing topics before they take off. Its paid features also include trend forecasting, where their machine learning algorithm predicts how a trend will grow over the next 12 months.
- *The Digital Native* by The Z Link (thedigitalnative.substack.com): This is our very own newsletter, which dives deep into internet trends, especially those related to marketing and social media culture. With a focus on Gen Z, you will receive two issues per month deconstructing a current trend and analysing why we think it is on the rise, what it means for our generation or internet consumers in general and any further insight we can draw from it based on our experience in this space. Not to be confused with:
- *Digital Native* by Rex Woodbury (digitalnative.tech): A weekly newsletter covering market trends and startup opportunities at the intersection of technology and people.
- *After School* by Casey Lewis (afterschool.substack.com): A newsletter with a loyal community of 30,000+

subscribers that keeps you up to date on everything happening in the world of internet culture and youth trends, in a simple and quick format gathering the latest updates you need to know.

Short-lived fad or opportunity worth exploring?

When we think of trends that seemed more promising than they ended up being, there are usually some common patterns that we can spot, which is why many of the experts I spoke to brought up the NFT boom as an example; it comes to mind immediately. Elijah Gray, an entrepreneur and interdisciplinary creative, points out that 'usually, a short-lived fad burns bright but burns fast, attracting everyone like moths. Everyone knows about it, but it eventually loses its novelty.' In his view, long-term opportunities are steady: 'They see smaller signals of growth but they're consistent. They don't need the world to talk about them because the few that are, love them.' If you want to spot sustainable opportunities, they will usually be found beyond the point where everyone is talking about them. For example, AI in itself is not really a trend – everyone is currently talking about it because it is a technology that is quickly rising and has potential to affect the way we do a lot of things. The fact that AI has reached the mainstream conversation does not make it a short-lived fad: the difference here is that the opportunities can be found beyond the wider conversation within this space, in the use cases that not everyone is talking about. That is where you can dig deep to find a problem that can be solved in a new way.

The NFT trend also had this element of 'get rich quick', and usually, when the mainstream conversation around a trend seems to present it like that, there is a lot of noise or misinformation involved. It is very, very rare to find a real get-rich-quick scheme. There is usually a lot more than what meets the eye, so be aware of when a trend is being presented as too good to be true. That is often a sign that it might be more of a short-lived fad than a viable long-term opportunity. The GameStop short squeeze in 2021, for example, illustrates the potential pitfalls in a lot of get-rich-quick opportunities as it was one that was definitely presented as such. While it allowed some early participants to make huge profits, the type of frenzied hype and surge that surrounded it led to a lot of latecomers facing significant losses as the stock plummeted from its peak. This view was shared by all the experts I interviewed. Lena Grundhoefer, founder of Zeitgeist Labs, who has done a lot of work in the areas of crypto and digital assets, points out that no trend is entirely transparent, so you need to approach the ones that appear to be so with caution: 'There is always more to understand beyond the surface,' she says. This perspective is crucial for discerning between valuable opportunities and mere hype, so rather than making rash decisions and jumping into something that seems like an obvious good opportunity, consider how it relates to all the above characteristics. Is everyone talking about it, a bit too quickly? Are people in the industry making promises that sound too good to be true? Is there clarity and simplicity around the problem it is solving and the way it is achieving that, or is confusion the general sentiment?

Recognizing trend cycles

An example of something that started off as a trend and ended up proving to be a successful long-term opportunity is wearable tech. Starting out as a niche type of technology, it then began diversifying to cover a wide variety of different consumer needs: fitness trackers, smart clothing, jewellery. There is enough space in the market for different companies to each capture its own specific segment: Oura for those interested in a more discreet wearable which has all the basic tracking features you need; Whoop for those more focused on in-depth fitness tracking; Apple Watches for anyone looking to benefit from a wider variety of features and apps; and lots more. The range of diverse consumer needs in the wearables market helped fuel innovation to cater to these different audiences, leading the technology from a niche trend adopted by a more tech-savvy crowd, to a mainstream and fast-growing market. This also happened during a time where health and wellness as a whole was growing as a trend, so technology that enabled people to stay on top of their health metrics more easily was very welcome. So why did wearables succeed? It was a combination of good timing, growing industry trends, wide consumer demand and sustained innovation that helped the trend of wearables get to where it is today.

There are a few specific elements we can recognize that made it into a successful opportunity. First, wearables aligned with *real* consumer needs and a type of lifestyle that was becoming increasingly important to a large amount of people. Health and fitness tracking, something that used to be done manually by a small tech-savvy crowd, had no reason being so inaccessible. It could make a huge difference in people's lives if they knew what affected crucial parts of their everyday life such as sleep, stress or exercise; but there were no good mass-market ways to achieve this. In my opinion, it was only a matter of time before tech emerged that aimed to simplify and popularize that process. Improving sleep, managing stress and measuring vital metrics such as heart rate were things that were becoming consumer needs, and wearable tech was a great solution. Seamless connectivity was another consumer need that played a part – wearable tech that achieved everything else but lacked this feature would not have worked well with most consumers, who need the simplest way possible to connect their devices to each other and create an easy-to-use ecosystem. This need for seamless connectivity is what partly led to the next reason this trend succeeded: market maturation.

A crucial phase that indicates whether a trend is here to stay is when the market starts to 'mature', so when established companies enter the market, in this case Apple and Samsung with their smartwatches. This type of recognition and investment into a trend validates it even further as a sustainable opportunity, and pushes it into the mainstream. When major companies enter a market, it is usually a good sign that they are making a very thoroughly researched and calculated decision, which points to the fact that a market is likely to be here to stay, or is at least an opportunity worth exploring at this moment. There are exceptions to this rule, as occasionally established companies take a risk by entering unproven markets (as seen with the 2024 release of the Apple Vision Pro, despite the fact that VR remains a niche sector).

Then, we have diversification. It is more likely that a trend will prove to be successful when there are diverse audiences and needs to target within it, rather than one broad audience segment. The range of different consumer needs in the wearables market created multiple different niches that brands could target in drastically different ways. This presents a lot more opportunities for brands to build in-depth solutions for their chosen segment, catering to specific needs and preferences. Targeting a very broad market and trying to meet everyone's needs is rarely a sustainable opportunity. Instead, when a market presents this type of diversification, it leads to diverse opportunities within it. So, when evaluating a trend that seems promising, an element to examine could be this: is this type of tech/innovation/solution trying to meet everyone's needs at once or does it target the specific requirements of a smaller segment that is more likely to be looking for exactly this? It is often better to offer a perfect solution to a segment of people, than to try to offer an average solution to everyone. This approach creates stronger customer loyalty and community, reduces competition and provides a quick feedback loop as a more defined customer base can offer more detailed and clearer feedback. Of course, there is a risk here of being too niche, and being in a market that cannot sustain growth in the long term. The ideal balance is one where your idea manages to successfully capture a segment by meeting people's specific needs, and can then consider adjacent segments to expand into and grow in the long term.

Just as we can observe what led to the growth and success of the wearables industry, there are more patterns that have been observed across trends that help to evaluate how viable an opportunity is, based on historical data. Learning to understand trend cycles can help you figure out whether an industry or trend you are considering is here to stay – and it's not as complicated as it initially sounds. One of the most long-standing theories that has been used to understand whether a type of innovation is here to stay is Everett Rogers's diffusion of innovations theory. It explains how new things spread through society and cultures, so evaluating trends in relation to this theory can provide some insight as to what phase they are at. It applies to anything from new ideas, technologies, behaviours and trends in general. The theory splits consumers into five groups:

- Innovators: Prone to taking risks and very open to new ideas.
- Early adopters: Well-connected and often seen as thought and opinion leaders, this group adopts new products right after the innovators and love trying new technologies.
- Early majority: This group is not the first to adopt new ideas, but they do so before the 'average person'. They usually need to see some evidence that a new idea is worth trying before adopting it themselves, so it takes some time for them to get there.
- Late majority: A sceptical and conservative group of consumers that will only adopt a new technology, idea or innovation after the majority has done so. They tend to be more cautious with new purchases and ideas.

- Laggards: The last group to adopt a new product or innovation, typically risk-averse and not fans of change. They may dislike change so much that they want to keep relying on traditional solutions and products until those are no longer available.

So, how does this theory help us understand trends in action? When we look at the example of wearables, which started out with a small group of innovators, essential in initially defining the technology, we can see the different phases: early adopters were crucial in building awareness and credibility around the trend, and showing how it could be integrated into daily life. Then, once the early majority started being interested it was clear that wearables were beginning to enter the mainstream market – a great sign that they were here to stay. This phase pushes companies to work towards better prices, as well as clearer, more accessible solutions. Now that the technology is established as useful and credible, the late majority is starting to adopt it as well, needing no further convincing of its value. As of early 2024, it seems like we are transitioning into this late majority phase. Evaluating a trend on this scale is a very tangible way of seeing exactly where it stands, and where there are opportunities for improvement. Based on the different types of audiences adopting a new product or service, entrepreneurs, marketers and innovators can evaluate which direction they should move into. So, if you were currently looking to launch a business in the wearables space, for example, you might start looking at what it usually takes for the late majority to adopt a product – is there anything that can be done to make it more useful and interesting to them that current products are not achieving, for example lower pricing or simpler features? Alternatively, you could think of what products or services would still appeal to early adopters in the space – maybe specific apps or accessories?

If you were evaluating another industry or niche, this is still very useful: if a product or idea you are looking at seems to still be in the 'innovators' or 'early adopters' phase, that means that it could have high potential but also high risk, and that its success would depend on whether it can cross over to the 'early majority' phase. If it seems to be in the 'early majority' phase, it usually means that it is a good time to enter that industry and find opportunities within it – the risk is lower and the potential is high. If an industry seems to be in the two later phases, then it may be an oversaturated market, providing less of an opportunity for growth. In that case, opportunities can be found if there is a way to rejuvenate and refresh an industry or trend when it has grown stagnant. If not, then you are better off looking into something else.

Another trend cycle theory that helps evaluate whether something is a long-lasting opportunity or just a passing fad is Gartner's Hype Cycle model. It suggests trends go through the following five phases:

- Technology trigger: When a new trend or technology first appears and there is a lot of attention and excitement around it – for example, when VR headsets first came out there was a lot of hype and talk about how they would change different industries.
- Peak of inflated expectations: The hype-peak of a trend, when everyone is talking about it and it seems to have

almost unrealistically high expectations around it – for example, the hype phase we discussed above related to NFTs.

- Trough of disillusionment: The trend doesn't meet its high expectations, and excitement starts to fade because people are disappointed. For example, when people realized VR was going to be too expensive and inaccessible, and it made people dizzy while using it so the experience wasn't as fun and exciting as originally expected.

- Slope of enlightenment: The stage where more realistic expectations are emerging about a trend, with people getting a better understanding of its capabilities and limits. Practical uses of a trend are being established, such as VR in high-end gaming or professional training simulations.

- Plateau of productivity: The trend becomes mainstream or is adopted by a wide audience as a common solution in its established area, with people now familiar with it and its proven worth.

Evaluating a trend based on the Hype Cycle can show you whether it is a viable opportunity: in the initial stages of excitement (the first two stages), a lot of the hype is often built around expectations and not based on facts or proven value. Be cautious of whether a trend is still in this phase, and try to see whether the excitement around it could just be that: expectation without much practical proof behind it. During this phase, trends often seem very promising and it is easy to be misled. Remember that this phase is still very uncertain, so hype does not equal opportunity. The 'trough of disillusionment' phase is a trend's reality check, where it has to prove whether it actually has enough applications and demand for it to be a sustainable opportunity. If it survives this phase and proves that it has real benefits and opportunities, passing on to the 'slope of enlightenment' phase, this is a sign that it does have lasting value. If it passes on to the very last stage, then of course you can tell that a trend is indeed here to stay. Using the Hype Cycle can help you evaluate a trend beyond the initial excitement, which is crucial. So many startups fail because they jump into something solely because of the hype, with no further evaluation, only to see that something ended up having no real-world benefits or applications or that it was way too niche.

Evaluating and using marketing trends

When our generation hears the word *trend*, most of our minds go to marketing trends: a TikTok trend that seems to be appearing in every second post you see during its moment of popularity, the memes shared between friends, a common language and the phrases we start to use without noticing it. These types of trends are relevant here because if you are working for yourself as an entrepreneur, content creator or something in between, understanding marketing trends and their cycles is crucial. Marketing trends are not only relevant to marketers, they go far beyond that. Whether we like it or not, we live in a time when the internet is one of our biggest assets, and more often than not, that is inherently tied into business and our careers. As we covered in the previous chapter, personal branding and content creation can skyrocket your career to new levels and offer unprecedented opportunities, and understanding marketing and social media trends is a huge part of that.

One result of social media is that trend cycles have shrunk to often just a few days. In the past, marketing trends could remain relevant for months – today, that is incredibly rare. Bite-sized content has made it so that trends come and go in days, maybe weeks at best, and their window of relevance has become smaller than ever. Everything is more ephemeral, and that can be difficult to navigate. We need to be more agile and adaptable than ever. For brands, this is often where things go wrong: 10-step approval processes to post any type of content on social media and jump on a trend result in them missing its window of relevance. That has the opposite effect to what they were aiming for: in an attempt to be seen as relevant and relatable by social media users, they end up being called *cringe* (our generation's ultimate mark of disapproval). So whether you are marketing your startup, freelance business or creating content for your personal brand, navigating marketing trends is a skill that won't go to waste.

Jamie Gilpin, former chief marketing officer at leading social media tool Sprout Social, says: 'Being active on TikTok is necessary job training for any marketer regardless of tenure or job title. Immersing yourself in the trends as a consumer is the only way you'll be able to identify relevant trends and turn them into equally relevant content.'[4] This belief was also shared by other marketing and community experts I spoke to. Janice Cheng, community lead at Aavia and brand marketing expert for Gen Z consumer apps, told me how she stays on top of marketing trends and evaluates whether they are relevant: 'I honestly look at what my friends and I share in our group chats. Sometimes it feels so separate, but I'm starting to realize that it is not separate at all. Seeing what my friends send me is a really strong indicator of what gets people talking, at least to evaluate a trend's *shareability*.' In marketing, the 'shareability' of a trend is one of its most telling qualities. Something that gets people talking is usually a trend worth exploring. Those trends are the ones that make it into real-life conversations, and beyond the screen. When marketers and creators evaluate trends, it's important to move beyond superficial metrics like view counts. Just because a trend is gathering millions of views on TikTok does not mean it's a marketing opportunity – instead, Cheng points out that the strongest indicator is comments, providing solid proof that something kickstarts conversations and engagement.

A big part of being able to understand and navigate marketing trends online is achieved simply through being a social media user yourself. That is why Gen Z can easily recognize when a trend is not considered relevant any more, without necessarily being able to put it into words – such as when corporate accounts on social media start joining in on Gen Z memes in a way that feels a bit forced to the audience they are trying to reach. Much of this process is an unspoken language, an inherent understanding that comes with being a Gen Z user of social media. So, use that to your advantage. The fact that social media is a great marketing tool that can unlock a world of career-related opportunities is a lucky coincidence happily co-existing with the fact that our generation of digital natives can make smart use of something we got to understand without trying. This is of course not to say that everyone is a social media marketer just because they're part of Gen Z; but it is to say that Gen Z is at least well positioned to comprehend the nuances that define social media trends and virality, which are so hard to explain to someone not deeply acquainted with them. So, as in Cheng's case, the best way to navigate social media trends and become better at using them is by simply looking around and observing our community. Your group chat, your friends, the things you respond to can all help you measure the relevance of something and come up with ways to use it creatively.

Navigating social media trends also does not mean jumping into every trend you stumble upon just because it seems to have potential. Successful social media marketing combines what is trending and what makes sense for the strategy and goals of the brand or the creator. Jumping into every trend as an attempt to reach virality will dilute the image of the brand or creator you are trying to market, and have a counter productive effect. Some of the most successful examples of brands intelligently taking advantage of trends have been discreet yet effective: it is all a matter of being attuned to internet culture and the subtle shifts that are always taking place. For example, when TikTok decided that the 'coastal grandma' aesthetic was its new trend of the month in May of 2022, fashion brand J.Crew discreetly jumped on the bandwagon by using the hashtag #coastalgrandma to promote some linen pants that fit into the aesthetic. The brand's chief marketing officer, Derek Yarbrough, reported that their post using the hashtag was one of the pieces of content with the highest engagement that month.[5] This type of marketing was smart: it did not rely on any big investment on a specific trend that could end up not working out for the brand, but instead found a small way to incorporate a current trend into social media content. Minimal risk, high reward. I asked Janice Cheng how she knows when a trend will work out for her brand, Aavia, and when it won't. After excitedly attempting to jump on viral TikTok styles like brands posting daily vlogs and day-in-the-life videos, and seeing that they were not getting the expected engagement, Cheng realized that these trends did not make sense for Aavia's audience. Aavia, a hormone health-tracking app, has a loyal community of users that absolutely love what it does, but it appeared that vlog-style content and TikTok trends were not resonating with them. 'Our audience doesn't need a vlog from us – they can get that from someone else. I realized that what they really want from us is science-backed, trusted, comprehensive education.' Their attempt was to go for aspirational lifestyle content, while their audience was looking for educational content. Experimenting with trends and coming to that realization helped the brand understand exactly what their audience wanted to see and market their product in a way that resonated with the right community. It is easy to find yourself in a bubble of exciting trends and ideas that sound great but are ultimately not right for the community you are trying to speak to. So, not every trend is for everyone, but experimentation can be essential in helping you figure out what people respond positively to. Figuring that out is where the opportunities lie. By figuring out that educational content is what their audience wanted to see, Aavia could then come up with creative ways to jump on social media trends that could be approached from an educational angle.

Understanding trend cycles and evaluating whether a trend is here to stay is a skill that will help you invest your time and resources in the right opportunities. The vast majority of startups and attempted businesses fail, and a small minority survive and thrive. To build a career working for yourself, knowing what is an opportunity and what is just noise will be one of the most essential skills in your toolkit – it's what will increase the likelihood of you being in that minority. Tom Eisenmann, professor of entrepreneurship at Harvard Business School, points out that the reason most businesses fail is because they jump into creating a solution before properly researching and understanding customer needs.[6] It is easy to jump into something prematurely as a result of the hype and excitement that often surrounds a trend – now, your focus should be on evaluating whether a trend is indeed going through its hype phase, or whether it has proven value, using the strategies mentioned in this chapter. Using creative market research strategies and going one step further than traditional research tools will allow you to spot actual problems and create solutions that are based on market needs, not mere hype. Being early to a trend can be a great advantage – but being early to a trend not worth investing in can drain your resources and push you further away from your goals. And while analysis and research is absolutely essential, so is moving quickly. Being able to get things done quickly can set you up for success – it's a trait many people struggle with but that is shared by most successful people. You need to find the balance between being restrained and analytical in the face of trends and hype, and being prepared and agile in capturing opportunities.

Notes

1   Griffith, E (2015) Startups are failing because they make products no one wants, Fortune, https://fortune.com/2014/09/25/why-startups-fail-according-to-their-founders/ (archived at https://perma.cc/4PC8-NTQF)
2   Cote, C (2022) How to identify business & market opportunities, HBS Online Business Insights, 5 April. https://online.hbs.edu/blog/post/how-to-identify-business-opportunities (archived at https://perma.cc/UGA3-AN5X)
3   Ibid.
4   Gilpin, J (2023) On trend and on brand: Why harnessing trends is the future of marketing, Sprout Social. https://sproutsocial.com/insights/harnessing-trends/ (archived at https://perma.cc/H34L-3JY2)
5   Lieber, C (2023) How to keep up with TikTok's lightning-fast trend cycle, The Business of Fashion. www.businessoffashion.com/articles/marketing-pr/how-to-keep-up-with-tiktoks-lightning-fast-trend-cycle/#:~:text=Park%20said%20most%20TikTok%20trends,this%20trend%2C"%20said%20Panzoni (archived at https://perma.cc/YR7D-9HGB)
6   Eisenmann, T (2021) Why start-ups fail, Harvard Business Review. https://hbr.org/2021/05/why-start-ups-fail (archived at https://perma.cc/9WHJ-T7FJ)

CHAPTER SEVEN

Looking ahead

Most of this book focuses on what you can do today to start building a career on your terms and defining the priorities that matter most to you. But setting long-term goals and aligning your present actions with these long-term priorities can be difficult. For most people, deciding on what you aspire to in the long term and setting distant goals does not come naturally. It is easy to focus on taking action in the present and neglect looking at the bigger picture – it often feels like enough that your life is making you happy today and that you are managing to live based on your values and priorities. I can certainly relate to this: I struggle with long-term planning and optimize on making the present as enjoyable and aligned with my priorities as possible. Most successful entrepreneurs I interviewed for this chapter felt the same way – when asked about how they plan for the long term, they said 'I don't'! They all emphasized the importance of adaptability and agility over trying to plan and create specific results, so this chapter will focus on how to navigate that uncertainty and make it work in your favour.

But before we get into that, we have to talk about the responsible, practical answer to the question of long-term planning. In order to plan for long-term success, you have to understand exactly what success looks like to you (as you did in Chapter 2), and picture different scenarios to figure out what outcome and achievements would make you feel happiest and most fulfilled.

The FIRE escape

First, there is the FIRE movement, which stands for Financial Independence, Retire Early. People with FIRE as their goal spend their early career years focusing on extreme savings and frugality, so that they can retire early and enjoy the rest of their life by living off the savings they have accumulated. The FIRE movement follows a strict savings programme, so those that want to adhere to it make career decisions heavily centred around this: they might, for example, favour a job that is more laborious and stressful for most of their career, if it allows them to comfortably stick to their savings programme, which allows them to retire early. This plan can sound appealing to many, while others cannot imagine waiting for their retirement to start making the most of their income and investing in themselves and an enjoyable everyday life. There is no right or wrong approach, you just have to recognize where you stand on this spectrum, which will help you make long-term planning decisions around your career. Are you more inclined towards living in the present and making the most of your young years, or are you happy to work for the sake of your future self, giving up more in the present to ensure you can give yourself what you want later on in life? If you choose the latter and lean more towards a FIRE lifestyle (with the goal of retiring by the age of 40), then you will have to plan for maximizing your income while minimizing your expenses.[1] Such a plan requires strict economic discipline through the years, and it will guide a lot of your life decisions, likely affecting areas like where you live, whether you own a house and the activities in which you partake.

The activist

Another scenario that might appeal to you is focusing on social change. For you, an ideal future could look like one where you are a successful activist working to create as much positive social change as possible. If this is your driving force, then your decisions when planning for the long term would be different as well. When choosing a job or starting something of your own, you will always need to evaluate whether it is aligned with this larger long-term goal. Every stepping stone in your career can be a valuable learning experience, and it is rare to have a whole career that fully aligns with your values and long-term goals. But the fact that this is a priority for you means that it should be front-of-mind when evaluating career choices, collaborations and next steps. In that case, you might want to consider starting side projects that align with this goal and which might open the necessary doors for you to achieve it later in life, prioritizing social impact over financial rewards or flexibility in the career choices you make. Once you become confident that you know what those long-term priorities are for you, no one can make you question the choices that make up your everyday life, because you know that they align with your personal values and are leading to the future that is right for you.

The entrepreneur

For others, their ambitions go beyond personal fulfilment or freedom, and beyond social change or activism, to goals like building a business empire. There are many personal, societal and financial reasons behind why people dream of building business empires and set long-term priorities that revolve around ambitious entrepreneurial goals and achievements. One, of course, is because some people want to achieve levels of wealth that are only realistically achievable by running businesses. It is no secret that wealth is what drives a lot of people to pursue entrepreneurship; which includes accessing the opportunity to invest in new ventures, philanthropic efforts and thus multiplying impact or supporting innovation. But there are many other reasons too, such as the unique challenge that pursuing a passion to such an extent can bring.

Entrepreneurs often aim to build empires in fields that they are highly passionate about, wanting to maximize the potential for the impact they can make within an area. Others embrace the challenge of achieving something that very few people have managed to achieve, aspiring to leave a lasting mark on the world and be remembered. Such a challenge also contributes significantly to personal or professional development and growth, and finally allows entrepreneurs to create opportunities for others too, generating jobs, contributing to economic growth and inspiring next generations of leaders through mentorship and guidance. So, for those with long-term goals like building a business empire, the decisions they make in the present also have to align strictly with this goal. Since it is so rare to achieve this, the choices they make have to contribute to their professional and personal growth significantly. The connections they make and opportunities they manage to access are more crucial, and they might give up priorities like starting a family in favour of advancing their career while they are still young, leading the way to creating greater entrepreneurial impact. All three of the scenarios mentioned are of course extremes. In most cases, you would likely fall somewhere in between, but they serve well to illustrate the different directions you could take.

From big goals to small steps

No matter which scenario you fall into or whether you're somewhere in between or far from these examples, understanding your long-term priorities and goals is the first step. Having reflected on your personal definition of success, it's time to try to get more specific with it: can you visualize where you want to be in five, ten or even twenty years? What does your ideal day-to-day life look like at each checkpoint? What kind of work are you doing? Allowing yourself to actually spend some time exploring that vision, maybe writing it down so it becomes more tangible and detailed, will make it all a lot clearer in your head. Keep your values in mind while doing this: do you know what your core values are? Understand what matters most to you in life (freedom, security, creativity, innovation, impact, something else?). What feels most aligned with who you are and who you want to be? Once you are clear about that vision, it's time for the next step: setting goals, big and small.

I've always struggled to set defined goals, always leaning towards abstract, unmeasurable goals. But I've managed to overcome this with the SMART framework, which stands for Specific, Measurable, Achievable, Relevant and Time-Bound. This is a famous goal-setting framework that makes it a lot more likely that you will actually achieve your goals. Rather than setting a goal such as 'I want to achieve financial freedom', the SMART framework suggests that you have to define this goal further to make it specific and measurable: how will you know whether you've succeeded? What exactly does financial freedom mean for you in practice? Is it a specific amount of money earned per year or something like the kind of property you can buy? Is it a type of lifestyle overall, such as being able to travel x amount of times per year, being able to afford to live in your favourite city or having a certain amount of money left to save? Even though most of this chapter will focus on how you can not only deal with but ultimately embrace the uncertainty of long-term planning, setting SMART goals can be useful in maintaining a sense of control and direction. It can be an important part of keeping yourself organized, and getting in the mindset of thinking about your long-term priorities in a more structured way.

Work backwards so you can break down what this wide goal means in practice and draw out the achievements that are *measurable* and quantifiable. Making sure the goal is *achievable* means that it should be 'within reason', whatever that means for you – but this is the tricky part: we usually underestimate what is achievable for us and set smaller goals due to self-doubt and limiting beliefs. We see others achieve larger, more ambitious goals, but do not recognize that they could be achievable for us as well. While 'A' in the SMART framework tells you to give yourself a reality check, my view is that you should probably dream bigger and allow yourself to believe that larger goals are achievable. So when thinking about SMART, take the A as a reminder to not underestimate yourself and what you can achieve, because we have seen that the act of setting larger goals actually makes you more likely to reach them.[2]

Next, making your goals *relevant* means that they should align with your priorities and values, meaning you have a good reason to be setting this goal in the first place. And finally, making the goals *time-bound* is as crucial as making them measurable: if you do not know when the deadline to achieve a goal is, how will you work towards it? Deadlines have a lot more power than we recognize: they determine how fast and how efficient you will be in your work. Give yourself the necessary time to work towards your goals, but also be wary of not giving yourself a lot more time than you need. If you are someone who works best under pressure and gets things done when deadlines are near, you need to recognize that about yourself and consider that maybe setting a shorter deadline to achieve a goal will work better for you. Personally, I'm able to get so much more done when I set very ambitious deadlines.

For example, the same project can take you six months or one month, with the only difference being that you plan more efficiently and work in a more structured way because of the time pressure. When the deadline is shorter, you find ways to achieve your goals more efficiently, so keep this in mind when addressing the 'T' in SMART. Setting long-term goals is easier if you break them into smaller, actionable steps and milestones. After you turn your long-term vision into SMART goals, you will still need to break those down to more manageable steps, so that you can have a clear direction to follow. Ambitious goals become so much more achievable when you manage to break down the steps that will lead you there. So, take the time to reflect on your long-term vision, write it down, and then set specific and measurable goals that you will work towards, broken down into smaller steps and milestones. Here's what that could look like for someone whose long-term goal is centred around reaching success and financial freedom through entrepreneurship:

Long-term vision:

> In the next 10 years, I want to build and grow a tech startup that addresses a real and important market need. I want the startup to help me generate personal financial success and independence, and my work to allow me to live a comfortable lifestyle and support my family while having the freedom to pursue my passions, hobbies and other investments alongside it. It is aligned with my values of security and freedom.

Turning that into a SMART goal:

> I aim to found a successful and useful tech startup and grow it to a valuation of over $10 million within seven years.

Breaking that down into actionable steps and milestones:

- Years 1–2: Conducting thorough research, identifying a market where a viable product solution could be built, creating a detailed business plan, bootstrapping or raising investment, putting together a team that will help create and launch the product.
- Years 3–4: Focusing on market entry and growth: launching the startup to the market, acquiring customers and collecting feedback, experimenting with marketing and growth hacking strategies to increase user base and revenue quickly and find out what works best to grow the brand, and securing additional funding if necessary to help with scaling.
- Years 5–6: Focusing on scaling and expansion: expanding the product's offerings or entering new markets, driving further growth, working on building strong customer loyalty, considering strategic partnerships or

acquisition opportunities that could be explored in order to accelerate growth.

- Year 7: Through sustained growth, achieving a company valuation of over $10 million, and exploring options for next steps such as selling the company or exiting in order to realize personal financial gains. Reinvesting into lifestyle, passions or new ventures.

This is just an example of what it could look like to turn your long-term vision into actual time-bound steps that you can follow, to turn it from a vague and distant goal into a reality. This is how you work towards your long-term goals today, aligning your current actions with the things you want to achieve in the future. You have to reflect, plan and then act.

The art of not planning

Now that we've responsibly covered goal-setting and the case for knowing exactly where you are heading, it's time for the part where I tell you that most people don't know exactly where they're going, and that's fine. For this chapter I interviewed many successful entrepreneurs who are achieving beyond impressive feats, who I expected to tell me their secrets to long-term planning and how *they* align the present with what they want in the future. I hoped, as someone that has always been a lot more focused on the present than the future and often neglected long-term planning because of this, that those who are far more accomplished and wiser than me would have these answers. But the surprising part was that they didn't.

What I learned through my conversations with experts and successful people around the world that are living their dream lives is that they focus on building flexibility, adaptability and agility a lot more than on trying to plan where they will be in 10 or 20 years. Most ambitious Gen Zers I speak to seem to share this sentiment as well: in most conversations I have had about this, I was faced with the fact that so many people do not know exactly how they want their future to unfold – they recognize the uncertainty of the time we live in, and are open to things unfolding unexpectedly in directions they could not have predicted. It is true that many of us could have never predicted where we are today, five years ago. Very often, the things you are achieving today could not have been imagined by your past self, let alone set as goals; maybe because your past self would have thought they were unattainable, or because you simply had no idea how your passions, interests and the opportunities you accessed would unfold.

If I had set specific goals for myself five years ago, I would have genuinely aimed for a traditional corporate career, hoping to make enough money to live comfortably, and doing something I enjoy – I could have never imagined what I am actually doing today and what it has allowed me to experience. Is it possible that long-term planning puts us in too tight a box? For some people, it can feel like that. Our lack of knowledge of what the future holds, and our inability to predict anything with certainty or imagine where roads yet unexplored will take us, can lead us to set goals that are too confined. Using this personal example makes it easier to illustrate: if I had set my mind on something specific five years ago, I would not have started a company, I would not be writing this book, and I would not have had many of the most incredible experiences, opportunities and connections with people that I got in the past years as a result of my current work. Had I set specific goals for my career, they would have been set too early, and promising to strictly stick to them would have led me to a completely different life than the one I live today – I would have rejected opportunities that did not align with my plan, and perhaps lingered too stubbornly on paths that were not right for me, that were decided as a plan by a version of me that had yet so much to figure out and learn.

To an extent, I see myself similarly today: I have absolutely no idea what the next years will bring, so I don't try to predict what the version of me 10 years from now will want out of life. This sentiment was repeated across almost all the conversations and interviews I had about this chapter, showing me that it is more prevalent than I imagined. So, how do we navigate this? No one loves uncertainty, but it is everywhere around us. Especially in careers that are digital-first, everything can change from one day to the next, there are too many moving parts we can't control, like online platforms and regulations. Adaptability is increasingly important for our generation and it will continue to be one of the most essential skills we can work on.

One example concerns those who work with social media, whether in marketing or as content creators. Social media platforms change all the time, and shifts in algorithms can affect your work significantly as we have seen in many cases in the past. One such case was Facebook's decision to start prioritizing content from family and friends on users' feeds, over content from pages and businesses, which significantly decreased the organic reach of businesses on the platform. Those that were relying too much on Facebook to drive business and awareness were suddenly met with low engagement and minimal organic reach, and were only able to get their content seen by enough people by paying for ads. In order to adapt, businesses and content creators running Facebook pages were forced to get creative by diversifying their social media presence across different platforms, switching their content over to platforms like Instagram and TikTok to reach new people. That change requires a different set of skills, as the content can differ so much – so those who weren't able to learn and adapt would eventually miss out. They also changed their approach by creating Facebook groups and engaging with their audience more directly, rather than relying on pages that now were providing minimal reach, which required a different kind of work and approach to how they promote their content or business. It was either adapt and find new ways to win or be forced to pay for Facebook ads to get the results you used to get for free.

Another example is the current (at the time of writing) switch that is taking place on Instagram and TikTok, where content formats that perform best have changed drastically in a matter of months. While video content used to perform best on TikTok and photo content on Instagram, this has now almost reversed: it is nearly impossible for businesses and creators to grow on Instagram without posting videos, and TikTok is informing users that photo carousel posts get more engagement than video posts. Creators and businesses are having to adapt as algorithms change and experiment in real time, making it impossible to plan in advance. Continuous learning is the most beneficial thing they can do, so that as online platforms adapt and change, they can adapt and change with them. We live in a time where we almost have to run fast in order to be standing still – being static and stuck in our ways is not compatible with the very nature of digitally native careers. While we have so many options and possibilities that were not available to generations before us to build fruitful and fulfilling careers, they come with the cost of uncertainty and the constant need to adapt.

There are, of course, some best practices that businesses and creators can follow to minimize the risk of uncertainty and future-proof their work. One of the most beneficial and long-standing strategies in that regard is 'owning' your audience. To create your own corner of stability and control in the world of social media, owning your audience through more direct channels like email or a personal website means that no matter what happens with social media platforms, you will be covered. This is why a lot of businesses try to convert their social media followers into email subscribers – email will always be there, providing a direct line of communication that has not had any significant changes in years. Without social media platforms as intermediaries, creators and businesses can be a lot more secure that the audience and community they have built, and the work they have done, will not be wiped away with the change of an algorithm. Without being subject to the whims of platform changes, an email list remains a stable asset that will grow with you over time. Owning your audience is about diversifying and protecting your work. So, while social media is an incredibly powerful tool for building an audience, whether personal or for business, the volatility of social media platforms requires us to create 'bits of certainty' that will protect our careers and projects, and that is part of long-term planning. Even though you don't know how it all will turn out, taking these steps today helps future-proof your work and ensure you will not be exposed due to the uncertainty of online tools.

Future-proofing your career, today

If we can't always plan for the future and know exactly where we want to be, do we just not think about the future at all? How do we navigate the ambiguity and ensure that we are still heading somewhere good? We have to balance looking ahead with the fact that we often have no idea where our career and the world is going to be in 20 years, and that's fine. The best way to deal with this is to make sure the present is as aligned with your values and fulfilling as possible. Aligning everything you do today with the things that matter most to you is a safe way to ensure that wherever you do end up going, it will be good. As long as your present actions reflect your core values and wellbeing, you cannot be led astray. For this chapter, I interviewed Anne-Laure Le Cunff, a neuroscientist, writer and entrepreneur. She is the founder of Ness Labs, 'a learning community for people who want to achieve more without sacrificing their mental health'. The Ness Labs newsletter is read by nearly 100,000 subscribers, and it helps readers make the most of their mind, becoming more creative and productive. As someone so invested in productivity, neuroscience and mindful growth, with a community that includes thousands of entrepreneurs and creators, I was curious about how Anne-Laure approaches long-term planning herself:

> I personally think that nowadays, it's impossible to really know where your career is going. So instead of trying to cling on to this ideal version of what your career will look like in the future, I think it's really important to optimize for your wellbeing today. And this is actually a really good compass: if you're feeling alive, excited, you're working with the type of people who inspire you, where you lose yourself in conversations and you leave with more energy than you had when you started talking to them... Even if you don't know exactly where you're going, you can trust that you're in a path of personal development that is going to lead to somewhere interesting. Even if you don't know what it looks like!

So, focusing on feeling well *today* with the work you are doing is still taking care of your future needs in a way.

I don't think we should live only for the future: designing a career on your terms is a process where the reward is that your career can contribute to you feeling great today, managing to live a life you love today, and ensuring that you are creating a life that is fulfilling and aligned with your values and who you want to be. This movement of successful young entrepreneurs feeling the same way and prioritizing fulfilment in the present moment is interesting to witness; even though our generation has lived in a time of large financial uncertainty and ambiguity (which creates a part of us that wants to largely control, predict and secure the future), we also don't want to be sacrificing the present for a promise of future fulfilment. When our actions consider fulfilment and happiness in the present, being aligned with the kind of person we want to be and the values that matter most to us, it is difficult to go wrong.

Milly Tamati, an entrepreneur specializing in the future of work, and the founder of Generalist World, shared similar advice: 'I have a maybe contrarian take to long-term planning, because nothing in my life has worked out as I planned. Nothing, not a single thing. Anything that I thought was going to happen in five years, has not. But 99 per cent of it has worked out way better, as something that I could not have planned!' How many instances can you think of in your own life where the same applies? When I asked Milly how she ensures that her present actions will lead her to the 'right' place, she continued:

> My take on this is to get really clear on the things that matter to me, such as having a strong support system around me, having a healthy body and a healthy mind, and my hobbies; these things that are my core stability, they are the things that I never want to lose in my life. And then trusting myself in that whatever comes up, whatever opportunity, whatever challenge, I will have the agility and ability to navigate them. We could go into recession tomorrow and then my plans would be out the window; it's about knowing that I can navigate that.

Defining the *core stability* that you want to be constantly strengthening is the key. Cultivating and strengthening a good support system, a healthy body and mind will help you create that stability and agility.

It might not look like it has immediate results, but these are the things that will help you survive and thrive within uncertain environments and changes, so focusing on them today will have lasting effects. It might be more rewarding to focus on building that system of resilience and adaptability and aligning your actions and decisions with that than trying to control the outcomes of a future that is so uncertain and unpredictable. With this view, uncertainty becomes an opportunity. Since you're not closing yourself off from future paths that you cannot yet conceive of, focusing on aligning the present with your values and keeping the future more open and less strict presents an opportunity to open up avenues for creativity and unexpected paths to success. For example, exploring side projects alongside your main job and trying hobbies and activities in new fields puts you in a position where unexpected paths could open up, new passions could be discovered and new connections could be made. Rather than placing yourself on a strictly defined path, keeping your options open and instead placing your focus on making the present as fulfilling as possible opens a door for serendipity and unforeseen opportunities to enter your life. You don't have to predict and try to control exactly what the future holds in order to be successful.

Another thing you can do today to build the required agility and adaptability is to start focusing on continuous learning and developing an interdisciplinary skillset. Making time for learning to be an active part of your life will prevent you from becoming stuck in an obsolete area or job, and keep you moving and evolving. Many people stop consciously learning and trying to develop different skills and areas of knowledge once they get a job they love or reach a career point they are satisfied with. But lifelong learning is a tool for adapting to change and increasing the variety of future opportunities that could come your way. If this is not something you are currently doing, consider making time in your life to integrate it. An idea I have observed a lot of people implementing is setting up a 'learning budget' (both in terms of money and time) every year to dedicate to learning new skills and gaining knowledge in new areas. These could be purely based on personal interest or on potential industry trends.

The power of generalizing

As the founder of Generalist World, Milly Tamati has spent a lot of time observing communities of interdisciplinary people that embrace having a multitude of skills and passions. Her company supports and creates opportunities for these individuals, as she believes that there is so much potential in being interdisciplinary, but not enough opportunities for people with such varied skillsets to put them to action. Implementing lifelong learning as a conscious practice makes you a more interdisciplinary person and that has great benefits in the face of uncertainty. As Milly pointed out in our conversation, a lot of generalists go through the first years of their career experimenting a lot, trying out different jobs and areas and trying to find a way to really fit in. It can feel slow and confusing at first, but what she is observing in this community is that we are now seeing a lot of generalists as CEOs or in the C-suite in general, because the way the world is evolving highly favours interdisciplinary skillsets in positions of leadership. Those who favour continuous learning and embrace developing multiple sides of their skills and knowledge bring a unique perspective and approach problems in a different way, due to their variety of experiences. Milly highlights that 'at the start of your career it might not be clear where exactly you fit in, but in your mid- or senior career you will see how you are better off for having this diversity of experiences. Take the time to experiment, learn multiple things and treat your 20s as a research lab where you are the scientist'.

This is not a new trend: in *Range: Why generalists triumph in a specialized world*, David Epstein explores how a diversity of experiences and skills can lead to the highest levels of success and innovation. There is a strong conviction that specialization is the key to success, but the increased uncertainty and fast-paced change in the world around us is creating a shift where interdisciplinarity can thrive more than specialization. Epstein points out that while specialization used to serve us well in the past, it is not the case any more. To succeed today, we need to be able to connect concepts and ideas across disciplines, and have a range of experiences to deal with modern problems:

> Like chess masters and firefighters, premodern villagers relied on things being the same tomorrow as they were yesterday. They were extremely well prepared for what they had experienced before, and extremely poorly equipped for

everything else. Their very thinking was highly specialized in a manner that the modern world has been telling us is increasingly obsolete. They were perfectly capable of learning from experience, but failed at learning without experience. And that is what a rapidly changing, wicked world demands—conceptual reasoning skills that can connect new ideas and work across contexts. Faced with any problem they had not directly experienced before, the remote villagers were completely lost. That is not an option for us. The more constrained and repetitive a challenge, the more likely it will be automated, while great rewards will accrue to those who can take conceptual knowledge from one problem or domain and apply it in an entirely new one.[3]

Epstein's book helps people realize that, today and tomorrow, the most valued type of worker is one that can draw from multiple disciplines and areas, that is not tied down to one specific job description, but is more interested in smart, creative thinking and thus being able to solve complex problems. Understanding this is bound to make you a lot more adaptable to anything that is to come in the future of your career. *Range* also popularized the concept of being 'a scientist of yourself'. In the same way Milly Tamari suggested experimenting in your 20s as if you are in a research lab, Epstein explains that rather than expecting to find an answer to 'Who do I want to be?' and creating the long-term plans to match that, it is better to be a scientist of yourself. This is where you instead ask smaller questions that can actually be tested, such as 'Which among my various possible selves should I start to explore now? How can I do that?'

Taking this approach means that you will put your efforts into various experiments as the world, the environment around you and your interests change, and you will get to explore and observe yourself in various different contexts from which you can then draw knowledge and experience. Rather than assuming our identity has to be set in stone and predetermined for the sake of long-term planning, we know that our lives could take so many paths we can't predict. While short-term experiments can feel like failures, they are what will help us figure out the things we are very best at, and the paths that are the best fit for us. The risk of strictly sticking to specific long-term goals is that it could keep you from moving on from something that is no longer a good fit for you. Through *Range*, we learn that building the ability to adapt, pivot and acquire new skills can be more valuable than creating expertise in only one area. At the same time, depth of knowledge and skill is definitely still valuable – research just shows that it works best when combined with breadth of knowledge, often leading to far greater potential for innovation and success.[4] Interdisciplinary career paths are usually non-linear, and that doesn't mean that any time is wasted. Every experience contributes to lifelong learning, self-discovery and the accumulation of knowledge and perspectives that is one of the most valuable assets you can carry with you in an uncertain future and ever-changing landscape.

Networking

We should also recognize the power of networking in protecting us in the face of change. You've heard it all before – 'your network is your net worth' – but it's true here too: creating a strong network of people across disciplines, roles and environments can create a protective shield around you as the world changes. Building a network today can help you succeed tomorrow: it is another facet of long-term planning that you can address without exactly planning. The more you advance in your career, the more you will witness first-hand how the people you meet can completely change the course of your life in ways you cannot predict; you may already have countless examples from your own life to point to. Knowing a lot of different people and building relationships with them can help you access opportunities and grow in unexpected ways, no matter what direction the world or your career takes. A single conversation with someone at an event could lead you to discover a new area that piques your interest, which you end up building a startup in; a friend of a friend could point you to the perfect job opportunity during an uncertain time in your career; an online connection could help you navigate a career transition and share valuable lessons from having done the same. The ways in which meeting a diverse range of people can influence your career and unlock opportunities for you are endless. Networking can take many different forms, from in-person networking where you intentionally attend industry events, conferences or social mixers to meet people, to online networking where you connect with those who might be able to teach you something. Especially in online networking, there is nothing stopping you from 'shooting your shot' and meeting people with diverse experiences and skillsets. And it's a domino effect: everyone you meet and build a relationship with has their own network, which by extension becomes yours. (That's why personal branding is so important, because in the world of online networking, making it easy for people to associate you with the things you are interested in will lead to you being connected to the best fitting opportunities.)

Remember that it's not a one-way street: when you are a helpful person and you genuinely enjoy adding value to other people's lives where you can, the same will return to you. Building a network is also great because you can help others through the people and opportunities you access. So, even if you are introverted or prefer working alone, don't underestimate the incomparable power of having a large network. Make a point of becoming comfortable attending events and speaking to new people, building relationships and offering your help and support where you can; it is one of the skills that will serve you best throughout your entire career, and you will become well equipped to deal with any change in circumstances. Building a strong network is part of the core support system that will help you alleviate the stress that comes with uncertainty, allowing you to feel more confident that you can deal with whatever comes your way.

Wellbeing

Finally, what a lot of this leads back to is the importance of optimizing for wellbeing. Taking care of your wellbeing every day is more important than trying to plan for anything else in the long term and predict where you will be in five or ten years – none of that would matter if you were not feeling well and taking care of yourself. You can pursue ambitious career goals and balance multiple things without jeopardizing your health and wellbeing, and without burning out. Almost everyone goes through burnout at some point, and if you work for yourself, it is especially likely you will too – I don't know any entrepreneur who hasn't gone through it at some point of their journey, myself included. But that doesn't mean I can't give you some tips to mitigate that risk and keep you as focused on your wellbeing as possible throughout your career or entrepreneurship journey; the more you manage to implement, the better off you will be. First, no matter how ambitious your goals are, make sure to set clear boundaries. It is very common at the start of one's entrepreneurial journey to be working constantly, from the moment you wake up to the moment you go to sleep, and then just repeat the cycle. Try to remind yourself that taking time to rest is not only beneficial, it is *essential* for your success. Running on an empty tank 24/7 is simply unsustainable, and you will crash harder than necessary if you do not intentionally make time for rest and fully convince yourself of its importance. Most of the time, our work is not as urgent as we are led to feel. Yes, there are work emergencies, but more often than not the sense of urgency we create around our work is a false one (with the exception of some industries, of course). You can dedicate downtime to simply doing nothing (yes, that's acceptable), as well as to pursuing hobbies and passions and spending time on things that inspire and fulfil you outside of work.

Then, remember to prioritize and delegate. Tackle tasks with intention, not all at once, but by prioritizing the most important things you could spend your time and energy on. And as soon as you can, start delegating. If you're working for yourself in any capacity, freelancing or running your own company, one of the main things you will have to learn is that you have to delegate. You cannot do everything yourself, neither should you try to – working with people that are better than you at different things will directly contribute to your success. At the beginning of your entrepreneurial or self-employment journey, there will definitely be a time where you do take on more than you should; that is pretty unavoidable in this type of career, until you get something off the ground enough to be able to delegate. If you plan to run your own company, delegating tasks to other people will allow you to keep your focus on the things that have the greatest impact on your company's success, which you cannot do if you are busy dealing with every single small task. The moment your work is generating enough revenue to be able to invest in something, you should invest in people. This is one of the most central entrepreneurial lessons: get comfortable with trusting other people to take on parts of your business and give up the need to control every single aspect of it yourself. Delegating and prioritizing is, therefore, a form of well-being, both personal and professional.

Mindfulness

Practising mindfulness is one of the most essential things you can do today to ensure a happy tomorrow. The best thing about it is that there are so many different forms of mindfulness you can practise, so you can find the one that works best for you: meditation, yoga, journaling, deep breathing exercises or conscious reflection. I used to work with a CEO who had time blocked out on his calendar every week simply for 'deep reflection'. It is one of the most impactful things you can do, and yet how many of us actually take the time to consciously reflect during a busy week? One busy week brings the next, and before you realize it, you have been carried away by the wave of everyday demands and obligations, and cannot remember the last time you slowed down and checked in with yourself. Checking in with yourself is extremely important: it is how you will be able to evaluate whether you are satisfied with the path you are on, and be able to access any problems that are not immediately obvious.

Practising mindfulness will allow you to bring to your attention whether you are feeling stressed all the time and there are changes you need to make. There is no point building a career on your own terms if you spend every day in a rushed stream of anxiety: feeling good is actually a priority. Mindfulness will help you recognize early signs of burnout, and reassess your goals, actions and path if needed. Need some more convincing? The tangible benefits of practising mindfulness are ones that everyone should reasonably want to take advantage of: it can improve your creativity, focus, decision-making ability, reduce anxiety and make you more present in everyday life so that life does not slip away without you noticing, which happens a lot more than we realize.[5] It can even strengthen your immune system and lead to improved cardiovascular capacity.

After experimenting with different mindfulness habits for years, I found a recipe that works well for me: meditating for five minutes every single morning (my top tip is that if you do it before you actually get out of bed, you have a much greater chance of sticking to it), and writing regularly to understand myself better, reflect and notice patterns. Others swear by breathwork, doing daily deep breathing exercises that you can find for any occasion: there are breathwork techniques that immediately decrease stress, others that give you boosts of energy and others that help you find mental clarity and focus. Everything is freely available online, and it can take only five minutes of your day – worth a try. There is a reason why most successful entrepreneurs out there regularly discuss the benefits of meditation and mindfulness and how it has positively affected them; it is thankfully a trend whose popularity has only been increasing, with enough examples to convince others to try it too. If you have never been the mindfulness type, take some time this week to try out different practices, with an open mind, and see what feels best to you. Don't be discouraged if you do not see immediate results: the magic happens when you have enough faith to actually stick to it for a little while. You'll just have to trust me blindly on this one.

So, you now know how to responsibly do some solid long-term planning by setting SMART goals, but also how to *not* plan, and why you sometimes shouldn't. There is great value in keeping your future open and focusing instead on building adaptability, agility and creating a fulfilling and aligned present. You might be reading this book precisely because you do not exactly know where you want to be heading. What I learned through this process was that so many successful people out there that have created their dream lives do not know where they're heading either, which does not have to be stressful or a problem to fix. You can embrace this uncertainty and turn it into an opportunity to focus all your energy on creating the best life for yourself in every moment, aligning your work with the life you want to live and your core values. The fact that we don't know exactly what the future will bring should not cause fear, but bring excitement.

Notes

1   Kerr, A (2024) Financial Independence, Retire Early (FIRE) explained: How it works, Investopedia. www.investopedia.com/terms/f/financial-independence-retire-early-fire.asp#toc-who-is-fire-designed-for (archived at https://perma.cc/CN5U-MZ5V)
2   Locke, E A and Latham, G P (2002) Building a practically useful theory of goal setting and task motivation: A 35-year odyssey, *American Psychologist*, 57 (9), 705–17. https://psycnet.apa.org/doiLanding?doi=10.1037%2F0003-066X.57.9.705 (archived at https://perma.cc/M45H-36GG)
3   Epstein, D (2019) *Range: Range: Why generalists triumph in a specialized world*, Riverhead Books, New York
4   Ibid.
5   Kane, R (2024) 39 mindfulness statistics and facts to inspire your practice in 2024, Mindfulness Box. https://mindfulnessbox.com/mindfulness-facts/ (archived at https://perma.cc/RZ2K-HM95)

Conclusion

After reading this book, I hope you can feel confident that your career does not have to fit within the well-defined box of a traditional path. You might have to unlearn everything you have been taught about what your career should look like and how you should approach it. The truth is, most of us grow up with a pretty set idea of what our work life will look like, and tend to follow that without questioning it too much. Part of that is because of the lack of education surrounding alternative career paths, entrepreneurship and self-employment. If this book leaves you with one thing, I hope it is that creating a career that contributes to your happiness and fulfilment and allows you to live your dream life is not as inaccessible as you may have thought. Tackling a challenge as big as 'building a career you love' can seem intimidating, and it is, until you break it down and distil it into questions to ask yourself, and small steps you can take.

If you are a part of Gen Z, there is a good chance you can benefit from the digital native advantage without even recognizing it. At the time we live in, this is an invaluable asset. While digital-first careers are definitely not the only way to achieve what you want, they are a huge opportunity that our generation can access at its prime time, taking full advantage of it. The rise of digital-first careers has shown us that the internet is an unprecedented tool for creating our own opportunities, leading to careers and lives that were not possible a few years ago. The freedom, flexibility and ownership that we can access thanks to the internet and the doors that it opens for careers and exploring our passions is something no other generation has had the privilege of experiencing. It allows us to upskill, experiment, network and learn, at the tap of a finger – a playground of opportunity. In my case, growing up playing around with digital tools and developing skills that could later be used to craft a whole career directly resulted in me currently living a life I love at 24, feeling like my career is the greatest contributor to that and an invaluable asset.

Years ago, I used to think of careers more as a chore that had to be figured out, something that I would have to compromise on in order to make enough money to do the things that make me happy outside of work. Work-life balance doesn't really exist when our work and our life are inherently intertwined: our careers should be a source of fulfilment, whether directly through the work we are doing or through the lifestyle they allow us to create. As we covered in Chapter 2, the most important thing to start with is to reflect thoroughly on what success looks like to you, personally. Take the time to answer the questions, visualize, reflect on what you want your life to look like and what values and priorities you want to design your life around. Make sure to release any judgement or preconceptions you have about what your priorities should be: this is about you alone, and how you can feel happy waking up every day, thanks to the life your career allows you to live. Any definition of success that you feel pulled towards is valid.

Once that is figured out – and you can take your time with it over days, weeks or even months – it's time to get into the practical stuff: how to structure your career to achieve your version of success. Starting side projects or side gigs alongside a main job that provides you with security is a great way to begin; it can allow you to experiment with ideas and learn what you like, with minimal risk. And if you are able to jump straight into something instead, and are at a point in your life where full-time self-employment or entrepreneurship is already possible, then take that leap and have faith that even if something does not work out, you will get priceless lessons out of it that will never go to waste. In Chapter 3, we explored just a few of the hundreds of types of entrepreneurship opportunities that exist (and new opportunities are arriving each day). People like you achieve incredible success on a daily basis thanks to this world of opportunities that anyone can explore. Anything is possible: if your dream is to travel the world while working on something you love, hopefully the tips and examples in this book can inspire you to make that happen. It is important to unlearn and let go of so many preconceptions we all tend to have about what is achievable: so many of us think digital nomadism is inaccessible for the first years of your career, or that a 9–5 office job is the only way to go, whereas we have so many examples that point otherwise.

One of the biggest tools at your disposal is personal branding: use it to make social media a field of opportunities that automatically find you. Don't forget that a huge percentage of opportunities out there are hidden; they are not the jobs you will find on job platforms, but the opportunities that are passed from person to person by being in the right place, at the right time, and proactively connecting with new people. Whatever the field you want to establish yourself in, building a strong personal brand will allow you to stand out and use social media as one of your most indispensable assets. Personal branding is what has built so many Gen Zers' careers from the ground up, and the best thing about it is that it is free and accessible to anyone. You just have to face the fear of putting yourself out there. You also now know the basics of evaluating trends to know when something is worth your time – feel free to refer back to these principles and strategies each time you consider a venture that seems promising, and with each experiment, you will collect your own lessons and an intuition for spotting opportunities.

With all these resources at your disposal, the last thing left to do is to face the fears that may hold you back from taking a leap and doing something different. Hopefully, if you are reading this, you are already convinced that following an untraditional path is worth it; what is left, is getting started. A big fear that holds people back from taking action, whether it is starting something of their own or building a personal brand, is the fear of being judged or failing publicly. For what it's worth, I'll tell you that every single successful entrepreneur I have met and spoken to has shared the same fears. All of the people you see succeeding seemingly effortlessly, have had to face the same fears and doubts; building the confidence to deal with them is a conscious effort that takes time. Anne-Laure Le Cunff, the Founder of Ness Labs (who I interviewed in the previous chapter) has always been ambitious and a high achiever. Those who can relate to that will know the feeling of fearing public failure and underachieving. In Anne-Laure's words: 'For me, the idea of failing publicly was very difficult. I was trying to do things that made sense for my career, 'the right things'. And something I realized now that I'm a little bit older, is that nobody's watching that closely. Really, nobody cares! Nobody cares that I have failed a few times, that I had a couple of startups that didn't work out. I had worked on so many projects that were complete failures. Nobody remembers, and I learned so much by going through these experiences. I wouldn't be the person I am today, doing the work I am doing today, if I hadn't gone through all of those experiences of failing and learning from those failures, and then growing thanks to them. So the one thing I would tell someone who is on the verge and struggling with similar fears, is to literally just do it because nobody's watching that closely.'

If you struggle to internalize that and face these doubts, just think of your own self: do you judge strangers, acquaintances and friends that take the initiative to put themselves out there and take a risk to create something? Do you judge those who are brave enough to start a project that later fails? Hopefully, you don't – instead you admire them for the risk they took, rather than judge them for their failure. Most people won't think twice about your personal branding content, your public efforts, your expression of your passions and interests. They will likely either scroll past, or admire you for putting yourself out there, maybe feeling encouraged and inspired to do the same. In this day and age, who's judging others for starting their own businesses and posting about it? Everyone is busy with their own lives, so you focus on yours. The fear of being judged and failing publicly will truly fade away the more you practise facing it – take it from me and everyone else who gradually took that barrier down by feeling the fear and doing it anyway. If it's hard, just keep reminding yourself why you are doing it.

There is also the fear and self-doubt around whether you are capable of achieving success and whether the risks and challenges you will have to endure are worth it. Jeremy Linaburg, founder of Wholesome Media, struggled with these doubts too before starting his company, even though he knew it was what he wanted to do. 'I just thought that I am so young, there is no better time to take a risk, even if it's scary. Why not try out something that I can test just to see if it works out or not?' Risk is not inherently bad, and experimentation will always result in some type of valuable lesson. In Jeremy's case, knowing he was young enough in his 20s to take risks and have plenty of time to recover if his venture failed was a comforting realization. But even if you aren't in your 20s, you have more time than you think. Even if you try out something and it doesn't go well, you have enough time to do something else.

Maura McInerney-Rowley, the founder of Hello, Mortal, dealt with this doubt by seeing how her work was helping people. If you are considering working on something that helps improve other people's lives, seeing their reactions to it can be enough to help you deal with the constant questioning of whether it is worth pursuing. Speak to friends and acquaintances that could find what you are doing useful, and that can provide you with all the validation and support needed to take the leap and keep going. And don't forget imposter syndrome – feeling like you are not qualified enough to do what you are doing, or like you do not really deserve your success. Almost everyone deals with that, and you would be surprised how many experts and seemingly successful and confident people still struggle with imposter syndrome; it is one of the most consistent doubts I see in the world of entrepreneurship. Funnily enough, no one knows what they're doing as much as we think they do. Everyone is just figuring it out as they go along. Maura reminded me that 'imposter syndrome makes us feel like we need to be complete experts to start a business, but you become an expert, there is never really a perfect time to start'. And it's true: most 'experts' out there only became experts after taking a leap and creating something that would later position them as such. It is rare for a founder to really feel like an expert before they start; you just have to trust that you have enough skills to begin, and remember that the greatest learning experience is the act of going beyond your comfort zone and having to learn on the job. Jeremy Linaburg similarly told me that, in his experience, you still struggle with imposter syndrome even when you succeed, which, for most people, is true. Success and achievements can either mitigate the imposter syndrome or make it worse, but Jeremy pointed out that these persistent doubts aren't actually a bad thing, because they present a real opportunity to become better, improve yourself and walk out stronger. And that's always a good thing.

At the end of the day, you have to ask yourself what you actually have to lose by taking a leap. The fear of wasting time is usually exaggerated in our minds, as attempting entrepreneurial ventures or experimenting in your career is very hardly ever a waste of time. It is always a learning experience that, even if it fails, will leave you with tangible lessons to look back on. We learn much, much better from experience than from theory or from other people's lessons. The fear of losing invested money can also be mitigated by bootstrapping or beginning with side gigs alongside the safety net of a regular job. So, what do you really have to lose by trying? When you're young, you can easily bounce back from any 'wrong' decision (and in this specific case, it is hard for any such decision to ever be that wrong). The worst that can happen is that you spend some time, energy and money on something that fails, that you then gain valuable lessons from that you can integrate later on in your career and have a higher chance of success. The best that can happen? You get to build your dream life through a fulfilling career that evolves in ways you never thought were possible or accessible.

And now it's time to talk about quitting. In *Range*, David Epstein writes: 'We fail tasks we don't have the guts to quit. Knowing when to quit is such a strategic advantage that every single person, before undertaking an endeavour, should enumerate conditions under which they should quit.'[1] You first need to let go of the belief that quitting equals failure. I hope the discussions around failure in this book have urged you to reframe the way you think about failing. Pivoting and quitting are central elements of entrepreneurship and self-employment. Many of the most successful startups you know today, pivoted drastically at some point in their journey. If they hadn't, they would have failed. Pivoting means being able to recognize when an idea is not working any more or is not needed by the market, and being open to changing it, even if you feel like you have invested too much into it. Clinging on to something because you have invested too much time or money in it is not a good strategy, and it can lead you to drag out something that is not working, wasting more time and missing valuable opportunities. There are cases where you do need to persevere, and cases where you simply need to quit or pivot. Did you know that the original idea for Instagram was for it to be a location-based app for checking in and making plans with friends, with gamification features, called Burbn? When the team realized that this idea drove minimal user engagement, and was too crowded with features users did not seem to care about, they decided to take a simpler approach and focus on photo sharing.[2] Had they not pivoted from Burbn to Instagram when they realized there was a much better opportunity at hand, they would not have had their $1 billion Facebook acquisition just two years after launching, and we would not have one of the most widely used apps and social media networks today. Another example is Slack, the online communication and collaboration platform used by thousands of teams and companies around the world. Did you know it was originally meant to be an online multiplayer game called Glitch? The game was particular, including messaging, collaborating and problem-solving features for users. When the team realized Glitch was not going to take off, they decided to focus their efforts on a different project: they had built a communication and collaboration system for their own use, and thought it might be useful for other companies too; and so, Slack was born.[3] Fast-forward to 2019, Slack had an IPO valuing it at over $23 billion, making it a massive success story and the fastest-growing business app of all time.

A lot of the biggest success stories in business are a result of being comfortable with 'failure', admitting when it is time to quit and pivot. If you are not comfortable with failure, you are setting yourself up for more of what you fear. So, how do you know when to quit? Besides the obvious signs of a failing business, there are the signs of when you should quit for personal reasons, admitting to yourself that something is not a good fit and is causing you more harm than good. Anne-Laure Le Cunff's strategy, informed by her experience in both neuroscience and years of entrepreneurship, revolves around noticing when negative patterns are repeating. 'It's completely normal to have days where you wake up and dread doing any work, that happens. But if it's been a few weeks in a row where I wake up in the morning and dread working on my stuff, then there's a problem there. Once you have noticed that there is a problem, you can start to diagnose it, understanding why you are feeling this way. Sometimes it is not the work itself, but the way you are approaching it. That could be a number of things: the people you are working with, the way you are organizing your time, the fact that you have too much going on, or the beginning of burn out. Sometimes it is something more fundamental, a sign that you are ready to move on to the next stage of your career, that you have outgrown your current work or projects, and that is completely fine as well. It's not easy, but it is about reflecting and staying in touch with your thoughts and feelings, and paying attention to signals that show it might be time for you to change something.'

First you have to consciously understand that something needs to change, and then figure out what it is. It is normal to never feel absolutely sure about the nature of that change, but it is like a muscle you have to train: pushing yourself to move forward and experiment, and learning that things will be okay.

Finally, I want to leave you with one suggestion: take action and stop overthinking. You have heard this one before, but in careers and entrepreneurship (like in most areas of life), perfectionism is an obstacle. There is an interesting leadership principle called 'bias for action'. Any time someone asks me what I consider the biggest indicator that someone will be successful, my answer is the same: when they have a bias for action. This refers to having a mindset or approach that favours taking action over inaction, without waiting for the perfect conditions to make a move. People with a bias for action are comfortable taking calculated risks, aiming to learn from the outcomes and adapt quickly. Waiting for the perfect conditions, the perfect moment, in order to take action, can be destructive. Learning to embrace the simple act of doing things instead of overthinking can push your professional and personal growth forward faster than anything else. There are millions of incredibly intelligent and skilled people out there that have big ambitions but don't meet their full potential because they never learn to act, remaining stuck in their heads and fearing change and failure. Having a bias for action is also like a muscle: the more you learn to simply get things done and execute your ideas the moment you have them, the easier it will become. Having a bias for action gets you out of analysis paralysis, the state of overthinking every decision and possible outcome and becoming stuck in endless loops of inaction.

Every time I had an idea for my company, a new direction we could move into or a way to experiment with a new offering, I usually took the first step in executing it right when I had the inspiration. Inspiration is fleeting, and you should capture it while it's there: it can lead to your most fulfilling and productive work. So when I was inspired by an idea or experiment, after a reasonable amount of consideration and long before reaching analysis paralysis, I'd simply start implementing it. Some of them stuck around, some didn't, but it is what led to most of the opportunities and growth I have had in my career. Reach out to that professional connection, shoot your shot, send a message suggesting a collaboration, set up a landing page, a social media account for your side project, anything. Any step is a step; any action is better than inaction. Become comfortable with uncertainty and recognize that success includes discomfort and doubt, but that it doesn't have to stop you from going out there and trying. What's the first step you can take today towards something you have been thinking of doing? It's time to close this book and go take it.

Notes

1   Epstein, D (2019) *Range: Range: Why generalists triumph in a specialized world*, Riverhead Books, New York
2   https://medium.com/international-school-of-ai-data-science/the-tale-of-burbn-to-instagram-a9035df134b6#:~:text=Rewind%20to%20the%20March%20of,%2Dbased%20check%2Din%20apps (archived at https://perma.cc/YTU3-Y8CH).
3   https://pixelpricess.medium.com/the-story-of-slack-9a92aa3771a1#:~:text=The%20startup's%20founder%2C%20Stewart%20Butterfield,companies%20went%20bonkers%20for%20Slack (archived at https://perma.cc/69YG-9U28).

Index

Looking for another book?

Explore our award-winning
books from global business
experts in Skills and Careers

Scan the code to browse

www.koganpage.com/sce

Also from Kogan Page

ISBN: 9781398613911

ISBN: 9781398613058

ISBN: 9781398609327

ISBN: 9781398613706

www.koganpage.com

Printed in the USA
CPSIA information can be obtained
at www.ICGtesting.com
JSHW071703251124
74283JS00014B/563